The Freeing of One

Billion Souls

Brent G. Maupin

Third Printing

ISBN: 978-1-7362258-0-6

TABLE OF CONTENTS

The warrior is always awake, even when he seems asleep. He is aware and on the lookout for the enemy, so that others can be less encumbered to do their part in God's Plan.

Prologue

My name is Brent G. Maupin. In 1999, some 21 years prior to me writing this book, I was diagnosed with non-Hodgkin's lymphoma. Needless to say, at only 45 years old I was shocked. I think most anyone who gets cancer at a relatively young age would say the same. However, I felt very strongly that God had a purpose for me in this life, and dying of cancer was simply not it. Yet, there I was with two young children at home, wondering how to tell them that their daddy had cancer, and that the doctors said there was no cure. This book highlights the major steps that I had to go through in order for a miraculous God given healing to take place. I then tell how this journey played a role in God's plan for us to do our part in the Freeing of One Billion Souls by becoming who God made us to be.

Introduction

The Freeing of One Billion Souls

I first experienced the releasing of the one billion souls from captivity midway through my illness. At that time, I was living in our family home in Sedona, Arizona with my then wife and our two children. She was out of town with the kids visiting her parents. That gave me time to be with myself without any distractions and, of course, with God. Sadly, our marriage was not a good one, as we argued all of the time. The list of why it was not good is lengthy, and at this point in time no longer important. When the revelation of the releasing of one billion souls from captivity came, I was in our guest room. When there it felt as if I had my own space, one where conflict with my wife had rarely taken place. I clearly recall saying to God about my illness, "What shall I do?" This question was not out of fear of dying, as I had a profound belief in God and felt that he had a job for me to do.

As quickly as the question was asked, I had a vision of a plugged-up culvert, or roadside pipe. It represented me, as my soul was definitely plugged up with too much emotional upset from the years of arguing with my wife. The next thing I saw was that the culvert had moved to the other side of the road. In its new location it was absolutely clear and not plugged up!

Amazingly I could then see, and more importantly could feel in my spirit, millions and millions of souls rapidly flowing through me. My soul and my body were the conduit for their freedom! Each individual soul was so very, very anxious to get through to the other side that they hurriedly pressed tightly against one another. Their urgency was unparalleled as they excitedly and even frantically rushed to get through the conduit to the other side. I could feel what was sure to be millions and millions of souls passing through my body! For that moment I experienced what it was like to be in unity with my spirit and therefore with God and fully participating in his plan.

I now see this as being an active participant in the Body of Christ! As quickly as this experience came it was gone, but never forgotten. When a person experiences or has a revelation from God at the deepest level of their being it is never forgotten. It would be several years before I would once again experience the freeing of any of these souls from captivity, and then it would only be three.

At the time of my illness I had not attended any given church on a consistent basis, as organized religion did not speak to me, nor did I ever read the Bible. However, back then and now, I talked to and about God and the greater world or worlds that God has created just about every day. At one point in time, a couple of months prior to feeling the souls pass through, I had my first experience with the Holy Spirit. During the initial stages of finding out about the cancer I did exactly what the doctors instructed. They said they could not cure the cancer but could extend my life. What I did not know was that this would require undergoing a few years of on again and off again chemotherapy treatments that could eventually kill me before the cancer did. This was no way to live, even if it would have given me a few more years, had I chosen that route.

After my first several rounds of chemotherapy my wife gave me a surprise party for my 46th birthday. That was very considerate of her. She had invited a few friends and co-workers of mine over. When it was time to blow out the candles, I took a deep breath and made a wish. My wish was that I would be healed of the cancer. Before I could let out the breath a distinct and precise wind came up from behind me. Crisply directed onto the candles it quickly blew them out. What was interesting was that of the dozen or so people that were there only one other took notice, my assistant from work, Barbara. We worked very well together. At one point in time, while going through the chemo, we had a discussion about my relationship with God and how I felt I had a purpose in life, but did not yet know what that purpose was.

She was so very supportive and said, "Maybe what you are going through is part of it."

As it turned out, she was very correct in her assessment.

This experience with the candles being blown out was when I became acutely aware of the Holy Spirit, as I knew it was indeed the breath of the Holy Spirit that blew out the candles. What I did not know was how it was going to go about fulfilling my wish to be healed. A few weeks later I had a CAT scan. I was told that the tumors had shrunk with the chemotherapy treatments that I had gone through. I was happy to hear this and it reinforced the fact that I had been feeling better. The severe pain in my abdomen had not come back for a few weeks. However, as the doctors said it would do, the cancer had started to come back. Hearing this news, I was disappointed, but I was not shocked. What it did was to make it clear that I was not yet to where I had to be to get through this most challenging trial in my life. In addition, the last round of the chemotherapy treatments had started to damage my heart. The doctors also said that the cancer would grow resistant to the treatments and as time passed, they would have to go to more and more aggressive treatments, which would damage even more of my organs. Thank God, God had something else in mind.

Chapter One

Experiences With God

My first conscious experience with the Creator of all things in the universe took place in my early thirties. Prior to that I think I did believe in God, but rarely had a discussion about there being such a deity. I certainly had not experienced God as I have now, and rarely if ever went to church. To me, there is a significant difference between believing in God and experiencing God. It's just my makeup. When I experience something so deeply it becomes very real for me. These experiences gave me the drive to get through the challenges of cancer, and give me the drive to keep going in my search for fulfillment of purpose. I had attended a few martial art tai chi classes and was doing a "standing meditation" exercise whereby you stand, often facing a wall, with knees slightly bent. I clearly recall that I was standing in the upstairs hall of our home in the San Francisco Bay Area. After a half an hour or so of doing this meditation I literally found a part of myself in the universe, and that I was one with it. I could see and or sense every planet and every star and everything in between. I knew that God was everywhere in the universe. Not a God out there somewhere, but a God that is within each and every one of us, and whom is present at all times. The Father of all creation is in everything and is everywhere, in every person, in every planet, every star, and every galaxy. He is an omnipotent, omnipresent God.

For those who are not sure about their beliefs in such a concept, or simply do not believe in God, he is still there in them, as God created them! He is the one and only true God.

> Saint Paul wrote in **Ephesians 4:10**, *"And the same one who descended is the same one who ascended higher than all the heavens, so that he might fill the entire universe with himself."*

Sadly, there is too much disbelief about whether or not what we call God exists. And too often the presentation of such a concept is in such a way that it turns people away. This is not because God is absent from us. It is because of our human error in the presentation and in our lack of knowledge of how the universe works. In this book I sometimes give what I believe to be constructive criticism of some beliefs and practices of the various Christian denominations. After all, there are about 33,000 different denominations of the Protestant Christian religion, and like all organizations developed by human beings, they are not perfect. Accordingly, there are 33,000 different interpretations of the Christian Bible. There are also about 22 different Catholic organizations, with the Roman Catholic Church being the most well-known.

As an example of the various interpretations of the Bible in the Christian religion, Catholics and Protestants alike, years after my experience with the one billion souls as described in the introduction I attended a three-day event where a prominent Protestant pastor was speaking. At one point in time he asked if there was anyone in the audience that had not been baptized and if not to please come forward. I had never been baptized in any church, though I clearly knew that I had a relationship with God and a purpose to fulfill. So, I thought what the heck, I did not want my pride to get in the way. I then walked up to the front. It was there that I and some others were, according to the pastor, baptized in the Holy Spirit. Yet, according to the belief of many denominations I have not been baptized at all, as they believe you are not baptized unless you go in complete submersion of the water. For other denominations you must go under three times, while others believe only partial submersion is required. While for others it is the sprinkling of the Holy Water onto the person. This is just one example of how various denominations interpret the Bible in different ways. So, I ask, which is correct? God knows, trust me, God does know. In this book I do not follow any given belief system from any specific denomination. The core of everything I have written is based on my first hand, one-on-one experiences with God through my spirit.

Based on the above, to many I may not be a baptized Protestant, but I have been blessed by the Holy Spirit, and that is all that is needed. I also know that God has been with me for a very long time, likely from the second that I was born and before.

> **Jeremiah 1:5 NLT**. *"I knew you before I formed you in your mother's womb..."*

Accordingly, God was with me well before I was baptized by the Protestant minister with what he said to be the Holy Spirit, which I do not doubt that it was. All of this being said, it is not my intent to offend any reader if they are a member of a certain denomination that believes in a certain way. But I do want to challenge that reader in a way such that by doing so they too will actively participate in the saving of one billion souls, regardless as to how I was or was not baptized, or came to believe in the power and authority that God, through Christ, has given each and every one of us.

Please note that throughout this text I will often use the word Christian. Yet nowadays many people do not use that term for themselves, and simply say they are "Believers." The term

Christian has unfortunately been tainted by too many mistakes made by those who profess to believe, but do not act accordingly. Remember, watch your actions as there are those around you who are ready to take note. If you see another Believer say or do something that you do not think is right, speak out! This is why God gave us a voice. Too often I see Christians speaking harshly about other Christians, and typically behind their backs. Trust me; doing so is an act of the enemy and not an act of God.

Gradually my awareness of what my life's purpose was began to unfold, and in the fall of 2015, I found myself for the first time regularly attending a local home church. This was over fifteen years after being miraculously healed from what the doctors said was an incurable cancer, which I will describe in the following chapters.

During my divorce we sold our family home. The fellow that bought it was a civil engineer, like myself, though he was by then retired. He wanted to talk to the fellow that built the home, so I of course obliged his request. We hit it off right away and almost instantly became very good friends. Years later, because of his wife's failing health, he could no longer attend church. Fortuitously, a pastor friend of his had moved back into town and was looking for a facility to start a new church. My friend offered his home, the very home that I had had the experience with the Freeing of One Billion Souls. It was because of my friend asking me to attend that I started to go to church on a regular basis.

Previous experiences of attending church had not done much for me. This one was different, as only about a dozen people attended, and we could freely participate in the discussions. After attending this home church for about a year, I was becoming more comfortable with talking to the pastor about my spiritual experiences and my miraculous healing, which are discussed in depth in the following chapters. I also purchased my first Bible and read it often. It was the New Living Translation and is what I use when various scripture is referenced in this book, unless noted otherwise. Learning about the life of Jesus was like reading a novel, especially when reading the Book of Acts, or the Actions of the Apostles. Eventually, I became comfortable enough with expressing myself that I wanted to tell the pastor about the experience I had had in that very home some sixteen years earlier when I had experienced the freeing of millions and millions of souls.

One evening I did mention the experience to him, but did not know how many souls had, or better said, were to pass through. I wanted to come up with a number as I wanted to better clarify the experience. During the same time frame I was wondering why it was that God spoke to me through my spirit so easily at times, while not so at other times. For example, in Lesson Two in the following chapters, I will tell how God spoke to me through my spirit and told that it was okay for me to love myself, and how important this was as part of my healing. At the time, I was very ill and my ego, or pride in Christian terms, was substantially diminished. Understand, I was bald from the chemo, including my eyebrows, and very thin from the illness. I was not very attractive! Yet, I so clearly heard from God through a greater me, which I now know to be my spirit.

I wanted so much to tell the pastor in 2016 what had taken place in that very same home, now my friend's house, back in 1999, and provide the number of souls that would be set free. I knew there were a lot, but just how many? I was also wondering why it was so easy for God to speak to me when I was ill but not later on. My thought was that my ego, back when I was ill, was substantially diminished and that now it had grown back to a degree significant enough to make this sort of communication more difficult. I substantiated this theory by comparing the first experience of hearing from God in the year 2000 when I heard, "Brent, it's okay to love yourself," to the second experience some two years later when I heard in not such a clear voice that, "The reason for your illness is now over." This I will cover more thoroughly in the following chapters, but the difference between hearing from God through my spirit the first time and the second, was that the second time it was more scratchy, as if I were listening to an AM radio from the middle of the ocean several miles off the coast of Hawaii.

Please know that when I say I heard from God it was clearly a greater me talking to me. It was my voice! But it came from such a very deep space, yet I knew it was from God! It was not until years later while watching a program called, "Father Spitzer's Universe" on Catholic television that it was verified that this is how God talks to us, through our spirit. That is why it was a greater me talking to me. The greater me being my spirit. My theory was that because I had felt so very good for quite some time my ego, or pride, had slowly returned and that it is what got in the way the second time that God spoke to me. Please realize that this shows us that our spirit is in complete and total union with God! So, in 2016 when I was searching for a number of how many souls had been released from captivity, I went home and for the first time intentionally put into practice the method of my theory for opening up myself to better hear from God.

What I did was to first put non-narcissistic love, or agape love, onto myself and onto my emotional body. I had practiced doing this before and is as described in Lesson 9 in the following chapters.

The feeling of peace that fills me each and every time I do this is so very wonderful. Also, and very importantly so, at this time I had been purifying my thoughts and therefore my mind for several days. Doing so clears the mind of any inappropriate thoughts or images that might come up from a movie, a sexually inappropriate conversation, or any other circumstance.

Purification of the mind from any and all inappropriate sexual thoughts has been practiced by many of the saints and I am sure several others throughout history. For me, it includes becoming acutely aware of not only every thought that I have had in this arena, but also of the short, mid and long-term impact that it has on the soul. Everything is energy, and the more energy sensitive a person becomes, the more effectively they can monitor any blockages. This is so very important, in fact purity of thought is the most significant portion of our spiritual quest. This is further discussed in depth in Lesson 7 and in Chapters 7 and 8.

Next came the third component of my theory of becoming better able at hearing from God. This was to disperse my ego to the greatest extent possible. I had been thinking about love and how it is key to all that we do in the spiritual realms. So, I then put the energy that comes from the thought of unconditional love, or God's agape love, onto my ego. The results were quite amazing. I could feel my ego being washed away. As I recall by this time, I was clearly in a deep meditative state. It was then, just as I was starting to drift off to sleep, that the words one billion came from my mouth. I was awake enough to take note, but not enough to become more fully awakened. I started to drift off again, and just as I was in that half-awake half-asleep space, when we are in the theta brain wave period, once again I spoke the words one billion! That is the number of souls that will be freed and return to their beginnings, to their Heavenly Father, or to God. Because of the events that are covered in the writings of this book, I have come to believe that all of the one billion souls will likely be given their freedom during my lifetime, yet I have no evidence of that. More importantly, is that God, our Heavenly Father, has a role for each and every one of us to play in the saving of these souls whenever that miraculous event does take place.

We participate in this process by being a conscious and active member of the Body of Christ, or as the Roman Catholics say, the Mystical Body of Christ. Even non-believers play a role. Theirs may very well be to challenge us who do believe in God so that we have something to be bold for!

> **Corinthians 12: 27 NLT.** *"All of you together are Christ's body, and each of you is a part of it."*

In **12:18** Paul says, *"But our bodies have many parts, and God has put each part just where he wants it."*

As members of the Body of Christ, each and every one of us has a place. It is not only our hearts desire but it is our duty to awaken to our calling and determine what is our position and function within the Body. To make a difference we must be humble in our thoughts and actions. And do not misunderstand, action is required. It is time to be bold in our calling and fulfill our duty.

Ephesians 2:10 NLT. *"...He has created us anew... so we can do the good things he planned for us long ago."*

By becoming who God made us to be we will automatically take on our role of being an active participant in this process. Being a member of the Body of Christ will not include being given orders from someone else, nor will it be like being a robot, or taking orders from some foreign God. It simply will be being who you truly are, who you've always felt you were, but until now had not fulfilled that feeling.

A Roman Catholic priest once said to me, "If you want to know yourself, get to know God." You see, God is the most amazing aspect of all of creation. After all, he created it! Our spirit is in the image of God, our heavenly Father! As we overcome most, and eventually all, of the limitations that society, culture, the enemy, and our upbringing has put on us, we will begin to understand what it is to be a full participant in the Body of Christ. We do this individually as far as our physical bodies are concerned. Yet, when we act, we do so in unison with the will and plan of the Father, through Christ. And just as God is within us, so is Jesus, but Jesus chooses when he will reveal himself. We are, in fact, to become like Christ.

To better understand God and Christ, and why Christ Jesus came, is an important step. To determine who these one billion souls are, we can ask what is it that keeps these souls in captivity, and how did they get there? The short answer is simple; it's just the way God our Heavenly Father created it to be. An attempt on the long answer is a bit more complicated. Are they the souls of the dead or that of the living? Soon after Christ's death, Peter states,

> **1 Peter 3:19-20** *NLT.* "*So, he went and preached to the spirits in prison-those who disobeyed God long ago when God waited patiently while Noah was building his boat.*"

Here Peter is speaking of the dead.

> **1 Peter 4:4-6.** Peter wrote, "*Of course your former friends are surprised when*

you no longer plunge into the flood of wild and destructive things they do. So, they slander you. But remember that they will have to face God, who will judge everyone, both the living and the dead. That is why the Good News was preached to those who are now dead-so although they were destined to die like all people, they now live forever with God in the Spirit."

Matthew 27:51-53. *"...The earth shook, rocks split apart, and the tombs opened. The bodies of many godly men and women who had died were raised from the dead. They left the cemetery after Jesus' resurrection, went into the holy city of Jerusalem, and appeared to many people."*

In the above, 1 Peter4:4-6, I know that many of my loving Protestant friends do not believe that Paul is speaking of those who are dead in body, but rather dead in spirit.

My Roman Catholic friends think differently and believe in purgatory, the place where the dead are purgatized, or purified, before they can reunite with the Creator. I go by what God through my spirit has shown me; that which I have experienced. As of now, my belief coincides with both the Catholics and the Protestants, as it can be both the living and the dead, which I will further explain in later chapters. However, to further my Catholic friends point from the book of John we read:

> **John 5:25-30 NLT.** *"And I assure you that the time is coming, indeed it's here now, when the dead will hear my voice— the voice of the Son of God. And those who listen will live. The Father has life in himself, and he has granted that same life-giving power to his Son. And he has given him authority to judge everyone because he is the Son of Man. Don't be so surprised! Indeed, the time is coming when all the dead in their graves will hear the voice of God's Son, and they will rise again. Those who have done good will rise to experience eternal life, and those who have continued in evil will rise to experience judgment. I can do nothing on my own. I judge as God tells me. Therefore, my judgment is just, because I carry out the will of the one who sent me, not my own will."*

Here, John is clearly speaking of the dead, and furthermore he is confirming the importance of doing "good will," which is elaborated upon in a later chapter.

During the process of becoming who we truly are, who God made us to be, and speaking what we know to be true, we automatically begin to better prepare ourselves to fully participate in freeing the one billion souls. Are we then not becoming more engaged as a member of the Mystical Body of Christ? Of course, as we are maturing in this manner. In doing so we can then better go about accomplishing God's work as he desires us to do. And remember, it is what we truly want to do as well, as it is our spirit in union with the Creator that desires to do the work. Then, if we feel so inclined to speak to others about the dead as John wrote in the above scripture, is this doing God's work? To me it is.

This preparation process is ongoing and has picked up momentum over the past few years, especially since the United States moved its Embassy to Jerusalem. To many, doing so is part of what sets the stage for what we call the Coming of Christ. What I have experienced is that this "coming" first takes place in us as it is God calling us and we are answering! When a revelation is received it is important to be bold and speak out about what it is you have received. Not doing so is not honoring God! He is calling us!

In **Ephesians 4:1-2 NLT** Paul wrote, *"Therefore I, a prisoner for serving the Lord, beg you to lead a life worthy of your calling, for you have been called by God. Always be humble and gentle. Be patient with each other, making* *allowance for each other's faults because of your love..."*

One aspect of becoming who God made us to be, and to answer this call, is to realize the various ways that Satan can or has influenced our lives. The enemy does not want us to answer this call. For example, though a small one, do you have a Facebook page? What image are you portraying with all the photos and travels? Too often, it is one that makes us look good in the eyes of others, rather than what the complete story of our lives. This is too often true whether we have Facebook or not.

In the Christian community we call this pride, though calling it ego is equally effective. We must become mature in our knowledge of the worldly ways, and how and why God has allowed both good and evil to exist. With our maturity we must also learn how to close the door to the devil, to seal off Satan's access to our life and to our world.

Ephesians 4:11-13 NLT. *"Now these are the gifts Christ gave to the church: the apostles, the prophets, the evangelists, and the pastors and teachers. Their responsibility is to equip God's people to do his work and build up the church, the body of Christ. This will*

16

continue until we all come to such unity in our faith and knowledge of God's Son that we will be <u>mature</u> in the Lord, measuring up to the full and complete standard of Christ." (underscored by this author).

Measuring up to the full and complete standard of Christ is a big calling indeed, yet it is what we are to do. As we get better in doing so, we become more adept in doing the Father's business, and help deliver these souls, whether they be the living or the dead.

In **Ephesians 4:8NLT.** Paul wrote, *"When he ascended to the heights, he led a crowd of captives and gave gifts to his people."*

It is my understanding that the captives referred to are those released from the dead as referenced in 1 Peter 4:4-6.

What is it that holds us back at this time from measuring up to the full and complete standards of Christ? It is our societal and cultural upbringing and the work of the enemy. Most all of us know there is an enemy but are unaware that there are indeed portals that gives him access to influence our world, and mind, thoughts, and decisions.

Romans 8:6 NLT. *"So letting your sinful nature control your mind leads to death. But letting the Spirit control your mind leads to life and peace."*

Among the several topics discussed and experiences shared in this book, the reader will learn to close these portals, how to close devil's door to our minds, which is part of our souls. Remember, the devil wants our souls.

The details that you will read in the following pages will show you how to find and how to close the gateways used by the enemy to access your life. This passage into our being is far too often achieved through our insecurities. It is really quite amazing how our physical environment interacts with the spiritual world, whether we know it or not. Learning such knowledge allows for us to become more informed and to then be able to become more Christ-like. Recall, for the forty days in the desert Jesus did indeed close off all access to the devil.

Ephesians 6:10-12 NLT. *"A final word: Be strong in the Lord and in his mighty power. Put on all of God's armor so that you will be able to stand firm against all strategies of the devil. For we are not fighting against flesh-and-blood enemies, but against evil rulers and authorities of the unseen world..."*

Having knowledge of this unseen world and how a portion of it works is important to more easily fight and win this battle. Remember, God never gives us a spiritual challenge that we cannot overcome. These battles challenge us and help to shape us to be more like Christ, to be more like who we truly are, who God made us to be.

By answering our calling, we are participating in the freeing of the one billion souls. By striving to become a better person we become a more complete version of ourselves. We will then automatically participate in the freeing of these souls. And trust me, they are very anxious for us to do so. They want to get out of where they are very badly. Some ask if these souls are trapped in a living person's body. I cannot say for sure but my impression is that they are of the dead. After all, in Ephesians 4:8 Paul did say Christ was leading a crowd of captives when he ascended from hell, and the one billion souls are captives! Surely, if the Body of Christ is being activated, we are in fact representing Christ in the flesh, to the best of our ability. If these are indeed the days of the second coming, then these souls are of the dead, and they are to be released by the Body of Christ, as Christ released the dead when he rose! From the Old Testament speaking of The Time of the End:

> **Daniel 12:2 ESV.** *"And many of those who sleep in the dust of the earth shall awake, some to everlasting life, and some to shame and everlasting contempt."*

Was the experience I had with the one billion souls a glimpse into the future? I say it was. Accordingly, becoming who God made us to be is so very important. We must be bold, as it is an absolute necessity to do so such that not only can these souls be free, but we can lessen the struggles that the rest of the planet will go through! This is a big deal!

The above being said, I want to share my background before getting into the intricate details of how I came to participate in the freeing these souls. This is so the reader can better understand the terminology that I use and the spiritual experiences that I have had. By profession I am a Civil Engineer. I am licensed in three states, California, Arizona and New Mexico. I am also an architect, and for about twenty years I was a licensed contractor in the state of California. As an engineer we are very analytical in our thought processes. We like to know how things work. Accordingly, our designs become better and better.

There are many lessons in life and sometimes they come in a manner that are at first difficult to understand. I have come to realize that the struggles I had in my failed marriage were simply part of the learning experience. Through the healing process, I put God's unconditional love onto my ex-wife, and myself. I did so as in my analytical mind it was a method by which I could move forward. It literally paved the way! At the oncoming of the illness, I had a profoundly strong belief in God and in his creation of the universe, and all forms of life in it. However, I had not yet experienced the agape love of Jesus.

God is in each and every one of us. For me to fulfill my purpose, he knew exactly what I wanted to learn, and how I needed to learn it. With all respect to my Christian brothers and sisters, my personal experiences with God as described in the following chapters did not include being pulled in one direction or another by any of the over 33,000 different Protestant denominations, the Roman Catholic Church, or by any other religious organization. I needed to learn straight from the source, like taking a class from the smartest professor in the university.

Prior to the illness, God our Heavenly Father, through my spirit, showed me many things in our universe. I had several experiences in the spirit and in the multi-dimensional worlds, including our own. Since my healing I have learned even more. I sometimes call what I went through when I was ill, "The Journey to the Soul."

For example, one of the very basic things I came to know about in the nonphysical world was that the soul of the dead, or what we call ghosts, do exist. I also experienced that often when a person commits suicide, their soul, or the ghost of who they were, often is left behind and gets stuck here on the earthly realm. With this, I then naturally came to know how to send them on their way, to the Light, back to God, or to the source if you prefer to use that title for the Creator of Everything. It is really quite straight forward; you simply command them to do so. If they are of the nasty kind and resist, then tell God to take them, and poof, they are gone! I also came to know that there are indeed demons, or spirits governed by Satan, that do their best to keep us from becoming who God intended us to be. By feeling their presence, I knew when they were near, and how to easily ward them off and send them on. From the New Testament:

> **Luke 9:1** *"One day Jesus called together his twelve disciples and gave them the power and authority to cast out all demons and heal all diseases."* and in **19:17** *"Lord, even the demons obey us when we use your name."*

> In **Luke 9:19 NLT** to the seventy-two disciples Jesus said, *"Look, I have given you authority over all power of the enemy..."*

22

From reading the above and based on my own experiences there is no doubt that we have the power and authority to heal the sick and cast out all demons. What many people do not know about is the portals that these evil doers use to access our world, believers in God and Jesus, or not. The books that I have read that do discuss the existence of these entrances do not give a complete picture of where these portals are hidden. In short, they are hiding within the glitches of our own personalities. Among many other things, in this book the reader will learn the knowledge needed to close the devil's door, thus allowing for them to leap forward in becoming who God intended them to be. That being a powerful, fulfilled, successful, and most importantly, a humble person. From the Old Testament about the story about Cain and Abel:

> **Genesis 4:6-7.** *"...then watch out, Sin is crouching at the door, eager to control you. But you must subdue it and be its master."*

This, my friends, is what we are able to do when we obtain the knowledge and have the tools and wisdom of how to close the door to the enemy. Doing so helps us to perfect becoming a better person, and we discover that, we then begin to help others, more and more. This can be done on the physical level, but as the reader will see, it also occurs on the supernatural or spiritual level, as the two worlds are connected.

Chapter Two

Nine Steps Towards Health and Enlightenment

The following gives a summary of each of the 9 lessons learned that were a part of the process that lead to my miraculous God given healing from cancer. The chapters following these teachings expand upon those lessons as I share my experiences with being present before Abba, our Heavenly Father, finding Christ by my bedside, casting out demons, and the significance of our dreams. We can then better become who God made us to be and then better go about completing God's business.

Lesson 1
Following Your Heart When in Alignment with Spirit

Soon after the Holy Spirit blew out the candles on my birthday cake, as described in the introduction, I was reading a book about how important it was to pursue the things in life that bring you great joy and fulfillment. I came to call this "Following Your Heart." During the time that I underwent chemotherapy I recall resting in the guest room of our home. I was doing my best to tune into why I was so very ill. It was then that I had the vision of a pipe, or culvert, on the side of the road, as previously mentioned. It was completely plugged, as nothing could flow through. I realized that this represented my connection or conduit to God. My spirit, infused with the Holy Spirit, was not able to flow through me.

I then asked God, "What can I do"?

As quickly as the thought entered my mind, the culvert was on the other side of the road, and flowing freely. What happened next was so very profound. I saw and felt millions and millions and millions of souls flowing as rapidly as they could through the pipe, which was a part of me, of my spirit in union with the Holy Spirit. From the New Testament:

> **Romans 8:16**. *"For his Spirit joins with our spirit to affirm that we are God's children."*

They were being freed from a place of captivity and I believe being directed or delivered back to the Creator, our Father Almighty, a reuniting with God!

As incredible as this experience was, I still found myself seriously ill. I knew I had to do something. It was a very arduous time in my life, especially with the marital situation. What I have learned is that far too often many of us tend to want to avoid conflict, and therefore say nothing. When in fact what we are doing is setting ourselves up for a much bigger problem further down the road. This was the case of my marriage. The problem was now much bigger and I was told that I had an incurable cancer. It wasn't long before I realized that moving out of our house was my only choice. It was by far the hardest thing I have ever done in my life. My children were 8 and 12 at the time. My love for them was so very strong, yet their daddy was dying. That being said, getting my own space was the right thing to do, as I figured that a part-time dad was better than no dad at all.

The lesson of following my heart played out over the next two years in a most extraordinary and often exciting way. This was especially true in my career as an engineer which I more thoroughly describe in later chapters. However, the impact of leaving the house that my children lived in is still with us, as children need both of their parents to live under the same roof, if possible. Looking back my wife and I probably made all the mistakes that could be made.

Lesson 2
It's Okay to Love Yourself

I found a small furnished apartment nearby and took out a three-month lease. On my first evening there I stood in the living room and felt into what was happening in my life. I thought of the hardships between my wife and myself, and could feel that emotional burden. It was like an energy that I could feel on the left side of my body. I then thought of the compassion I had received from one of the nurses during a chemotherapy treatment when I was undergoing such staggering pain throughout my torso. I felt that sensation on the right side of my body.

It felt so good thinking about it. I then thought, "What the heck, why do I want to think of the hardships?"

I then only thought of and felt into the feeling of the compassion. The more I thought of and felt into it, the stronger it became. Soon, I could feel that energy of health and compassion enter my body. Within seconds I heard what I now know to be my spirit, and I am sure in union with the Holy Spirit, speak to me.

It was a "greater me" speaking to me.

I clearly heard from deep within myself my very own voice say, "Brent, it is okay to love yourself."

This, of course, was speaking of a non-narcissistic love of self, or agape love. I was astounded to hear such a direct message! I wondered what this meant, as I thought that I did love myself! After all, I had graduated at or near the top of my class, I had had great jobs throughout my career, and as far as my children were concerned, a great family. But I was very ill and I needed to take note of such a profound message.

I was not knowledgeable of the Bible at that time. However, I knew that this voice was indeed a greater me, and that it came from such a deep and profound place. It was also as if the message was orchestrated by God, and that it was He that spoke to me. Not a God out there somewhere, but God inside of me. Years later after reading the Bible and listening to various Biblical studies I came to realize that it was my spirit that spoke to me, and that our spirit is in union with God. Often, I had difficulty explaining this to my Christian acquaintances, as they had not been taught this, and too often were taught that God is outside of us. This is unfortunate, as it presents a problem with speaking in a manner that encourages others to pursue Christ, and instead turns them away. Recall that the Apostle Paul wrote:

Romans 8:16 NLT. *"For his Spirit joins with our spirit to affirm that we are God's children."*

It was my spirit that spoke to me and the words were those of God, as He is in us and we are in him. It is important to know that God does speak to us through our spirit. Note that I did not say soul, as there is a difference between the two.

Thessalonians 5:23 NLT. *"Now may the God of peace make you holy in every way, and may your whole spirit and soul and body be kept blameless until our Lord Jesus Christ comes again."*
In **EPHESIANS 6:18 NLT** Paul wrote, *"Pray in the spirit at all times..."*

It is important to know that the Bible makes a very clear distinction between the spirit, the soul, and the body. My point being, it was my spirit in union with the Father that spoke to me. God speaks to us through our spirit. The Catholics understand this. Please note I am not a member of that religion, but I do watch their programs and read about their beliefs. What I have discovered is that there is much more to the Catholic Church than most Protestants and even the average Catholic alike understand about that religion.

From this experience of hearing God in this manner I did learn that on a subconscious level the ability to love myself had been blocked all the way down to the cellular level. This obstruction was put in place by the messages received as a child from my parents while fighting with each other. As children we absorb those messages and because of the imprintation they make on us we begin to think the same of ourselves at a visceral level. This is a very important lesson to learn. During the time when God spoke to me my mother was still alive. She and my father did love each other but they simply did not get along. Because of the profoundness surrounding me receiving this message I knew I had to speak to her about the way she had treated my father.

At the time confronting my mother was a very difficult thing for me to do, and had it not been for the cancer it was something I would not have done. Looking back, it seems so unlike me to not just come out and say what was on my mind, yet not doing so easily was the reality at that time. You see, a personality trait of mine was to avoid confrontation, and it was my upbringing from my mom when I was a small child that engrained that tendency into me. Thus, I was confronting the source of my anxiety.

I traveled from Arizona to northern California to see her. While sitting at the dining table I found the courage and asked, "Mom, why did you treat dad the way you did?"

She knew I was struggling to find answers in my life. I will never forget her answer.

She replied, "Son, if I have ever done anything that has hurt you, I am sorry."

She was so very sincere and meant every word. A huge burden left me. At the subconscious level the messaging that disallowed me to love myself immediately started to go away! A couple of months later I recall being in the lobby of my office building where I worked at the time. By then I must have shared this story several times. I was thinking about it once again when all of a sudden, I could feel the unraveling of this energetic blockage from the left side of my abdomen. Because of my mind working on and focusing in on this, my body was able to release the impediment right then and there. Looking back, perhaps I did not remove as much as I had thought of that messaging, but it was very significant and I certainly got enough out to move forward to the next several lessons that God had in mind.

Lesson 3
The Importance of Our Word

Fortunately, throughout my illness I was for the most part still able to work, though certainly not as efficiently as before. One morning when I came into my office, I found a book sitting on my desk. This was before I had decided to change careers.

The lady that cleaned our office knew that I was ill and she had left it for me. In short, it was a spiritual book that emphasized the importance of speaking your truth and how important our word is. It was not a religious book, but it had values that I believe aware Christians would agree with, and it certainly resonated with me. It was about the importance of our word and the power that comes when we speak the truth.

> **Matthew 12:36 NLT.** *"And I tell you this, you must give an account on judgment day for every idol word you speak."*

It is very important for all of us to understand the full depth of what Matthew meant by this. After all, in Genesis 1 it is clear that God created the earth with His Word and that Jesus himself is the Word Incarnate!

The information in the book I was given also emphasized the importance of asking for clarity when we communicate with others so as to avoid misunderstandings. It also spoke of not taking things personally. These are important lessons in life for all people. It is interesting how different teachings compliment the information given in the Bible. This being said, I believe it is also important that we do not confuse the significance of these writings with that of the ultimate message of the Bible. However, that is a subject for a different day. Also, unfortunately, the use of the Bible by too many has in fact turned many away from God by the way it has been presented. Many weaponize the Word self-righteously rather than use the Word to elevate in Love those they are presenting to.

> Continuing in **Matthew 15:11 NLT.** *"It's not what goes into your mouth that defiles you: you are defiled by the words that come out of your mouth."*
> **15:16** states, *"Don't you understand yet? Jesus asked. "Anything you eat passes through the stomach and then goes into the sewer. But the words you speak comes from the heart-that's what defiles you."*

Here, Jesus is emphasizing the importance of our word and what we speak. To be more precise, that which we speak and how it is spoken will define who we are.

> **James 3:2 NLT.** *"...For if we could control our tongues, we would be perfect and also control ourselves in every way."*

And in **3:5** *"...But a tiny spark can set a great forest on fire. And the tongue is a flame of fire...."*

John 1:14 NLT. *"So, the Word became human..."*

Most all people I know, even my Christian friends, do not realize the power of our word and the damage or the good that it can do.

Recently, I listened to professor Jordan Peterson from Canada speak on how political correctness was destroying his country. By elaborating on this subject, he was putting his job and his career on the line, as he had received two letters from the university where he worked at that time that demanded he stop speaking out.

When asked why he would place his livelihood on the line, and I'm paraphrasing, he replied "that he had no choice, as to not use the word that God gave us would allow for the enemy to win."

You see, we are not just fighting for our county and our society, but for our souls and for those around us. We must know the power of and use our word as God the creator of all things has intended! It is a very powerful tool. It is a co-creation with God for the transformation of the world around us. The Catholics and many of the

Protestants in the Word of Faith movement understand this, as well as others.

Lesson 4
Do Not Be Offended or Do Not Take Things Personally

Also discussed in the book that had been left on my desk was a discussion on not taking things personally by what others say or do. When we find ourselves being offended, even to a small degree, we have work to do on ourselves. If someone insults us, or as children if another child makes fun of us, we tend to take what was said personally. It is very important to learn not to do so. When we hold any kind of grudge towards others Satan gets a grip on us. As children when the teasing or actions were impactful this memory can stay with us for a very long time. This will in turn build into what I call a personality glitch, which I discuss in detail in later chapters. It is this memory and the emotional reaction that follows that can keep us from growing into whom God intends for us to be.

As parents it is important to understand these values and teach them to our children, so as to help our children grow into balanced and successful adults. As not understanding these values will allow for the devil to get a grasp on us. We become bitter and sometimes hateful.

Our words are then sharp and we in turn hurt others as we were. In doing so Satan increases his hold on society. Parents need to inform their children to not take things personally when another child teases or offends them. We need to show them how it is those kids who are acting out because they are jealous or possibly because they come from troubled homes. We must then show how to have compassion for those who would act out in that way, and to be confident in whom they are.

Human beings are God's children and he has shown us his teachings of the aforementioned in the scriptures of the Bible. At the time I went through my supernatural healing from God I was not reading the Bible. Looking back, he was revealing his truths to me in these lessons. We have all heard when Jesus said as written by Luke:

> **Luke 6:28 NLT.** *"Bless those who curse you. Pray for those who hurt you."*

To keep the devil from entering our lives it is important to listen to Jesus' words.

> **Matthew 5:43-45.** *"You have heard the law that says 'Love your neighbor and hate your enemies.' But I say, love your enemies. Pray for those who persecute you. In that way you will be acting as true children of your Father in Heaven."*

These are very important words and not only did they play a powerful role in my healing but continue to do so today, thus the writing of this book. Not only does following this lesson make you a happier and healthier person, it also allows you to become much more successful in fulfilling your life's purpose. Doing so pushes the devil out, and the tools to do so even further are discussed in later chapters.

Sadly, in today's society far too many people become easily offended, Christians and non-Christians alike. Though we need to strive to not be, sometimes there are times when you likely will do the same to someone else. As a Christian when you espouse your standard of morals and values others may take offense, even when your beliefs are being stated in a non-pretentious manner, and not being imposed onto them. The hot topics of today's society are Christianity, politics, homosexuality, and the LBGQ movement. In the political climate if we say we are conservatives many people get angry, and if the person we voted for becomes President, there are those who will riot and overturn cars. Why is it if we say we believe in traditional marriage we get labeled as a homophobe? When it comes to an angry and violent reaction, Satan has influenced these people.

Matthew wrote in **15:19-14.** *"Then Jesus called to the crowd to come and hear.*

"Listen," he said, "and try to understand. It's not what goes into your mouth that defiles you; you are defiled by the words that come out of your mouth."

Then the disciples came to him and asked, "Do you realize you offended the Pharisees by what you just said?"

Jesus replied, *"Every plant not planted by my heavenly Father will be uprooted, so ignore them. They are blind guides leading the blind, and if one blind person guides another, they will both fall into a ditch."*

So be prepared, as we strive to not be offended and become more of who God made us to be, we will often do so when we speak the truth, just as Jesus did.

Lesson 5
Ask for Clarification

It became clear to me how important it was for my word to be meaningful and to not take things personally. It was equally so to ensure that my discussions with others and theirs with me were clear and not misunderstood. There are methods that are discussed in various books that teach how to better communicate with each other. In this book I do not go further into this subject, but do stress its significance. When discussing important issues, especially with those who seem to disagree with you, ask for clarification and repeat in your own words what it is you think they mean, so that there will be no misunderstandings.

I cannot over stress the value of Lesson 3, The Importance of Our Word, and Lesson 4, Do Not Take Things Personally. That being said, Lesson 5, Ask for Clarification, is equally important as without Lesson 5, one cannot fully implement lessons 3 and 4.

Chapter Three

Forgiveness and the Final Healing

Lesson 6
Forgiveness

This lesson within itself is one of the most if not the most import of the nine lessons given in this book. Within a couple of months of reading about the importance of our word, I had a significant setback in my health. My strength was weakening and I was sure that there were some lumps under my arm pits. This was not good. I was surprised, as after having had such a powerful experience with hearing my spirit speak to me, I thought that likely healing had taken place. To the contrary, eventually I had difficulty walking up a slight pitch in the parking lot outside of the office where I worked. I decided to wait a week and see how I felt then. After one week had gone by, I felt even worse. I picked up the phone to call the doctor.

Then I thought, "What are they going to say?"

They are going to have me come in for an appointment. Then, they are going to have me get another CAT scan and then they are going to put me back on the chemotherapy treatments.

The memory of the last treatment was still with me where the chemotherapy started to damage my heart. My body told me so by the great anxiety that I felt during that particular session. The nurses were surprised that it was me that was reacting as I had, as apparently I was their ideal patient. I wanted that IV out of my system and I wanted out of that place. They offered a drug to calm me and I said, "You do not understand. I do not want this in my arm."

The anxiety that I felt during that last treatment was later confirmed when the doctor ordered a test that showed the damage to my heart. It was further verified by the great emotional relief I felt when the doctor said that to continue the treatments would do no good. Please recall that the type of cancer that I had was not curable. The chemotherapy would only extend my life, and even then, the quality would not be good.

I then set the receiver of the phone back down and said to myself that I already had decided not to go that route. I felt a very strong connection to God and equally felt that He had a plan for me, and this gave me strength to do so.

As it was near quitting time, I left work and went to the video store, as somehow, I thought a good movie would distract me from worrying about my condition. After walking through the aisles, I realized I had to do something and watching a movie to distract me was not it. I drove to the second apartment that I was staying at and parked in the driveway. I was desperate as the thought of telling my children that I was not getting well was more than I could handle.

I remember saying to myself, "Think of something! Think of something."

I then thought, *Well, when did the symptoms start?* I counted back, one, two three...then six weeks. *Okay. What happened then?*

It was six weeks earlier that my symptoms came back.

I next thought, *Okay, what happened six weeks earlier?* Thinking back, I remembered that my wife and I had held our first and only settlement conference with she and I and each of our attorneys present. The thought of the hurtful and untrue things that were said by my wife made me cringe. I was the only one of the four of us that could barely speak because of the emotional upset over her words. I was hardly able to hold back the tears. This is a good example of how powerful the spoken word can be when used for all the wrong, spiteful and hateful reasons.

I then thought, *Okay, now what?* I then realized I had to forgive my wife. She had to be forgiven for the hurtful lies she had told, the untrue rumors she had started, and for the personal verbal attacks made towards me, not only since I had moved out, but for what had been ongoing for years. The pain was so very great and the emotional wounds so deep I did not know if it could be done, as yet even today such horrible lies said by a spouse should not be repeated. Yet, not only was my life on the line, but the future of my children's lives was as well.

I sat there in the car and repeated," I forgive you Ann, I forgive you Ann, I forgive you." (The name has been changed.) I said this over and over again for probably an hour or even more. I would catch myself, wondering if I truly meant it.

I would then say to myself, "You mean this Brent, you mean this."

I knew I could fool myself but I also knew I could not do the same to God. After saying that I forgave her over and over again I then went into the apartment I was staying at and sat down on a reclining chair.

I tilted it back and continued to repeat, "I forgive you Ann, I forgive you, I forgive you." I said this time and time again, over and over again, knowing I had to truly mean it to the depths of my soul. Eventually, I fell asleep.

Drowsy, it was early morning, and the sun was starting to come up. I was only half awake but clearly felt a strong heat in my abdomen where the tumor was located. The heat was so vibrant I wondered if I was dreaming. I then saw an image of my sister standing next to me. Actually, it was more like knowing that she was there rather than actually seeing her. Accordingly, her spirit, in union with God, played a significant role in my healing. The interaction between her spirit and mine enhanced the heat. Her presence did not completely shock me, as she supported me in much of my healing journey, including accompanying me to see John of God, a healer in Brazil, which is a story for another time. As I began to wake, I realized the level of heat in my abdomen was quite intense, and not just in my dreamlike state. I wanted to prove to myself that I was in fact not dreaming. At the time I was having trouble with my right knee so I instructed the heat to go to my knee and heal it. To my surprise it did just that!

I then immediately said, "No, no. Go back to my abdomen," as the tumor was far more important than my knee! Once again, the heat moved to my abdomen. By then I was fully awake and soon enough the intensity of the heat dissipated, and shortly after that it was gone. I stayed in the recliner for a short while longer, and then stood up. I walked around the room. My strength had returned and my symptoms were completely gone!

Amazing, I thought! My trust in God and my gut feeling that he indeed did have a greater purpose for me was intact!

The act of unconditional forgiveness, or what some call radical forgiveness, is far more important than most of us realize. It does not mean that you have to like the person, be friends with them, or agree with how they conduct themselves. But it does mean that you have forgiven them completely and fully for the hurt they have caused.

> In **Ephesians 4:30** Paul wrote, "*And do not bring sorrow to God's Holy Spirit by the way you live. Remember, he has identified you as his own, guaranteeing that you will be saved on the day of redemption. Get rid of all bitterness, rage, anger, harsh words, and slander, as well as all types of evil behavior. Instead be kind to each other tenderhearted, <u>forgiving</u> one another, just as God through Christ has <u>forgiven</u> you.*" (underscored by the author).

If we harbor anger, we cut ourselves off from living a fulfilled life. Doing so squeezes down our connection to our spirit, and therefore to God, and this can be to the point that we are almost completely cut off from God. Therefore, we have removed ourselves from all that the universe has to offer us. By holding onto anger and bitterness we not only allow for the devil to get a hold of us, but open ourselves to sickness and ultimately death. The choices are clear. Which do you choose?

With all the above being said, my journey was not yet over.

Lesson 7
Purification of Thought

> **Luke 17:1 NLT.** "*There will always be temptations to sin.*" However, it is what we do with it after we sin that counts...*then if there is repentance, forgive.*"

Recall how in the first chapter I wrote about how important purification of our thoughts are? It is so very important to practice this lesson each and every day as not doing so will hinder our progress in moving forward to becoming who God made us to be.

In the spring of 2001, I had been feeling good for several weeks and I was in the beginning stages of starting a new and exciting project for my work. I had been asked by an old friend to help with the engineering and testing of a new structural steel connection that he was in the process of patenting. I was to fly to the San Francisco Bay area to meet with my friend and the fellow that would be helping me during the testing process. A few weeks prior I had moved into a nice condominium that I was renting. When I first moved in, I had turned on the TV and was surfing through the channels when I came across a movie with sex scenes.

I knew that it was not pure in mind for me to watch that sort of movie, yet there was a part of me that said, "Go ahead, what the heck, just for a short while."

After a while the movie was over and I turned it off. I knew that my actions were not in alignment with my desire to go deeper into my spirituality, to find God and to heal my body. I could even feel my abdomen twinge, as if something was not right. The energy in my body was off. For several nights before bed I would pray at my bedside, and do meditations, and then more prayers, and do "thought exercises" to cleanse my body. I did so whenever I felt a sexual stimulant as a result of a particular scene in the movie. I would immediately recognize it as a "bug" trying to bore its way into what I now realize was my soul, thus attempting to weaken my spiritual self and perhaps ultimately to even kill my physical body. I began to call these things "energy bugs" as they were not visible in the physical world. They had a tail that would vibrate and thereby continue the sexual stimulation that I felt. The intent was to cause a distraction from my awareness of the bug and then it would attempt to bore its way further into that particular portion of my soul.

I did these cleansing-purification prayers and meditation exercises for about six weeks. I would kneel at the side of my bed and focus on any stimulant that I sensed or on any area of my body, like my prostrate, that might be affected by such negative energies. It was key that I recognize the stimulant for what it was, and not let the sensation take me away into some sexual fantasy. This was not easy to do as in this day and age we are programmed to do just the opposite. I put my thought-energy directly onto the stimulant. Doing so disrupted the bugs' cover. I could then see it for what it was. With the force of my thoughts I would then push the bugs out of my energy body, or soul, one by one. They then could no longer continue with their evil task. I was quite surprised at discovering these "bugs" and knew that they were very real in the unseen world. I also knew they were a direct result of watching the highly inappropriate sex scenes in the movie. This was the devil at work.

Even with me successfully removing each and every "bug" from my being I began to feel ill once again. The physical weakness had returned along with the cancer-like symptoms. I was to fly to San Francisco, California to meet a fellow that was to work with me on the new project. I decided that I would make the flight, but that I would withdraw from the project when I arrived. I recall that shortly after I got to the shop, I had to walk up a rather steep driveway. I was so weak that it was all I could do to make it to the top, and that was with taking a break halfway up. Shortly after that I introduced myself to the fellow that I was to work with, John from South Africa. Nothing seemed out of the ordinary, and I decided I would wait until the next day to withdraw from the project.

Early the next morning I woke to a dream where I had climbed a ladder and reached a landing. The fellow that I had met the previous day, John, was just below me on the same ladder. I reached down, grabbed his hand, and pulled him up to the same landing that I was on. In the dream I had great strength and when I woke up, I was feeling exhilarated. I immediately realized that once again all of my symptoms were gone! Another piece of the miracle that ultimately healed me, as guided by God, had occurred.

Instead of resigning my position I met with the owner and with John and we planned the testing process.

That evening I flew back to Arizona. I got back to the condominium where I was staying, and went to bed. Early the next morning I had another profound, mystical experience. In a dream- like state, though I was basically awake, I found myself in a room about twelve feet square with a standard ceiling height. The walls were white but there was a stain on the lower portion of the walls, about two and a half feet up. By instinct I knew that the stain represented the dirt, or dirty water, that was there from watching the movie with the inappropriate sex scenes in it. The fact that the dirty area was now only a stain represented that what had caused it was now all gone, and that part of my soul was purified. The stain represented what had been there, not what was currently there. I then found myself in another room of the same exact size. This time there was no stain, but there was dust on the walls. The dust clearly represented that I had not been in that room, or better put, what the room represented, for a very long time. After experiencing this room, I found myself in yet another room, again the same exact size as the first two. This time, there was no dust or stain on the walls. They were pristine clean! I knew at once that I had not been in that space for a very, very long time.

Next, I was in the midst of the universe! I could see stars, but they were different than the stars that we see from Earth. I turned my head to see other parts of the universe and off in the distance I saw the most amazing planet. Rays of white light shot up from all around its perimeter, and when the rays from one side crossed over the rays from the other side, the light of each turned into a rainbow of light, and cascaded down onto the planet below. When I became fully awake from this experience, I knew that this planet was a very special place indeed. I later concluded that this is likely where the ascended masters reside, the home of the saints, and I thought likely the home of Jesus.

Years later, when I read the book Heaven Is For Real, where the little boy who had died and left his body came back and described Heaven as being covered with the light of a rainbow, my thoughts of how special this place with the rainbow light had been confirmed.

I will never forget this. Not only was it a profound experience that gave me insight into our soul and our spirit, but the next evening was my son's fourteenth birthday, and being healthy during this celebration was very important. I recall that there was a kid's event going on in town that we went to. Instead of being ill and wondering if I would have another birthday with him, I was well and strong. Since then, I have celebrated many birthdays with my two children.

The lesson here was clearly the importance of purification of thought, and how watching pornography can damage and lead to the death of the soul. It was later revealed to me that the soul is made up of our emotions and an aspect of our mind and/or our will, represented by the first and second room, respectively. Many of my friends, Christian or otherwise, often do not understand when I call the emotional part of our soul our energy body. I refer to it as this because I experienced this part of my being many times when going through my spiritual journey. The bugs I previously described were definitely attempting to bore their way into my soul. If successful, they could have caused illness to any specific part of my anatomical body by directly impacting the corresponding part of my energy body. When on our spiritual journey God shows us and challenges us with what we need to see and be challenged by when we need it.

Years later, I discovered that a continued purification process of our thoughts and therefore our mind cleanses every cell in our physical body. This is achieved simultaneously. Purifying the soul by the thoughts of our mind automatically purifies the body. This allows us to be more like Christ and allows for more of God to be in us, and we in him. This in turn allows for our prayers to more likely have an impact and be answered. This is a big deal.

Some sixteen years after the above described experience of seeing the rainbow light fall onto the planet, I was doing a focused mental purification meditation. I discovered that by focusing with my mind I was eventually able to wash away the effects of my life experiences, or sin, that separated me from God. Sin is not a condemnation from God, but is simply an act that separates us from God. I believe it does so through the processes previously described.

After going through this purification process for quite some time I had a vision of each of my children, then both in their twenties. However, in the vision each were very young. My son was maybe three or four and his mom was there. He had on a colorful pair of shorts similar to that which we bought him once when we went to Hawaii. Then, I clearly saw a vision of my daughter, even younger than what I saw my son as.

It was clear to me that each was in essence, born again. That is, given a new chance on life! That evening when I went to house church, I told the pastor and everyone else of this experience, explaining that through purifying ourselves we help our children, and we can better our chances of our prayers being answered. This is because we become more like Christ. Within the following two weeks, just as I was again about to enter our church, my son called. He told me of a profound experience that he just had and that he had asked for and received a sign that Christ was indeed who He said he was.

I walked into our church and told the pastor what my son had just said. This was an important step in my son's understanding of what I call real Christianity, not the one that has too often been portrayed with condemnation and flat out not promoting God as he intended it to be.

Also, over the next several weeks, there was a very noticeable difference in my daughter as well. Her speech and behavior changed. She started to call me more often, something that she was not able to do for years because of her ADHD. She simply was not comfortable talking on the telephone to anyone for any length of time. Her calls were now frequent, to the point of being daily. She even mentioned God on occasion in our conversations. Purification of our minds, bodies, and souls is of the utmost importance and starts with our thoughts.

Lesson 8
Love Others Unconditionally

After the experience of learning the importance of the purification of our thoughts I continued to be quite healthy. I went ahead with the structural steel design and testing project previously mentioned. We did this work in the laboratory at the University of Arizona in the Civil Engineering Department. The work there was quite involved and brought me up to speed with my profession as a licensed engineer, as up until then I had worked in construction management for most of my career. I now know that this experience allowed for me to more fully step into that which I was meant to be in my physical world, and that being a structural engineer, something I love very much.

Over a year went by before I had my next lesson from God. I was at the facility in San Francisco where I first met my friend John from South Africa, finishing up the documentation of the testing results. A friend had given me a book that was about unconditional love for others and for yourself. For several months I had felt quite well, yet that particular day I was feeling out of sorts. I had not been back to see the doctor for over two years. The memory of being ill was still embedded in my mind. Accordingly, whenever I did feel a bit off, I became alarmed.

After reading about the importance of love in this form, I went into my room to lie down for a nap. I closed my eyes and thought about what I had read. I then placed the "the thought of unconditional love" onto others I knew, especially those who had hurt me. At some point in time I added the word "energy" as there is an energy that emanates from our brainwaves that follows and reflects our thoughts. This is very important to understand, as our bodies respond to this. In my case it was the emotional body that responded, which is a part of our soul. As I recall I placed this form of agape love onto my ex-wife, her attorney, and anyone else I had come across that I had a dispute with. These were as close as I could come to having enemies. The same concept of our thoughts holds true with evil, or the lack of love. I am sure that those who study quantum physics would understand how our thoughts scientifically impact the world around us.

I then considered myself, and my emotional body, and how damaged it had been with all of the fighting between my ex-wife and I, back when we lived together. Words have power, as previously discussed. This power, if used with ill intent, can cause great harm to others. This is especially true when in continued proximity, and it does not get any closer than sleeping next to someone. I knew it was her words that had upset me very much, thus compromising my emotional body, and making it susceptible to illness. I also knew I had learned much from this experience and that God had his hand in this teaching from day one. At the time I did not read nor own a Bible. However, I knew that having forgiveness and blessing the best you can those that oppose you, was the right thing to do. I now see this confirmed in the Holy Bible.

> **Matthew 5:44 NLT.** *"But I tell you love your enemies and pray for those who persecute you."*

> **Luke 6:27 NLT.** *"But to those of you who will listen, I say, Love your enemies, do good to those who hate you."*

Romans 12:14 NLT. *"Bless those who persecute you, bless and do not curse."*

Romans 12:20 NLT. *"On the contrary, if your enemy is hungry, feed him; if he is thirsty, give him a drink."*

1 Thessalonians 5:15. *"Make sure that no one repays evil for evil. Always pursue what is good for one another and for all people."*

Looking back, it is good to know that I was with the will of God when going through my healing.

Lesson 9
Put Unconditional Love Onto our Emotional Self, Our Soul

Still on my bed and not feeling well, I continued to think of my journey, the illness, and of unconditional love, or agape love as I have now come to know it. I then decided to put that energy onto myself, and in particular onto my emotional body. Please recall that in Lesson 7, the Purification of Thought, the emotional part of my soul was as represented in the first room that I found myself in with the stains on the sides of the walls. This part of our soul is impacted by what we see, what we think, what others say and do to us, and more. Think about it, when we see something beautiful, we feel good emotionally. To the contrary, when someone speaks harshly to us we feel the impact of that as well, especially if we are close to them. While resting I specifically recall using the words "putting the energy of the thought of unconditional love onto my emotional body."

As discussed in the previous lesson, our thoughts do produce an energetic pattern, and so does our body. This has been proven in many scientific experiments and can be seen with the use of Kirlian photography. This form of photography is used to capture the phenomenon of electrical coronal discharges and was discovered by Semyon Kirlian in 1939. It accurately photographs the energy that emanates from various objects, including the human body.

Upon placing "the energy" of the thought of unconditional love onto my emotional body, I immediately felt a surge of healing flow through my body, in particular the part of my soul that was so badly wounded from too many years of a very bad relationship. It was then that my spirit spoke to me for the second time, some two years after the first which, again, was shortly after I had moved out of the house. Once again, it was a greater me talking to me. What I heard was, "The reason for your illness is now over." Needless to say, this was a profound moment.

As with the first time, I knew this was in fact coming from and in union with God himself. Recall that in Romans the Apostle Paul wrote:

Romans 8:16 NLT. *"For his Spirit joins with our spirit to affirm that we are God's children."*

I knew this voice, this feeling, this "knowing," was coming from my spirit. Yet, I also knew that it was as if it were coming direct from God himself. This was such an amazing experience! As I told others, my friends understood to the best of their ability and accepted this as a gift from God. To the contrary, some Christians that I knew would question my experience and the description of how God through my spirit spoke to me. Sadly, this type of judgment is common in various Christian communities.

Several years later, after purchasing and then reading my Bible, I was better able to put into words this experience, and include scripture as I have done in this book. God speaks to us through our spirit. Our Catholic Christian friends understand this, as well as some Protestants. It is our ego, or as my Christian friends say, our pride, that gets in the way and plugs up this process. After hearing those wonderful words, it took another year before I finally went to the doctor to get a CAT scan. It showed that there was "complete and total disappearance" of any and all tumors.

Looking back, I then thought; what had I gone through such that God would tell me I was healed by using the words, "The reason for your illness is now over"? Obviously, there was in fact a reason or a lesson and that I must have learned what it was. I then took note of the experiences and counted them. There were nine. Thus, the nine lessons described in this book.

This part of my journey was now over and the next phase began to unfold. What was interesting was that when God spoke to me through my spirit the second time, as described above, rather than being crisp and clear like it was some two years earlier, it was then a bit crackly, as if listening to an AM radio from way off in the distance. This is an important subject matter.

Consider that over the years I had often wondered why was there a "poorer connection to my spirit" the second time, as I had briefly mentioned in Chapter 1. Recall that to some extent my ego had made its way back into my being. Also, recall that when I first heard from God through my spirit telling me that it was okay to love myself, I was very ill. I did not look good physically and struggled emotionally with all that was going on. I certainly did not feel bravado by any stretch of the imagination. By the time He spoke to me again, to tell me the reason for my illness was now over, I was feeling good. Though I believe I am not an arrogant person, we all have an ego and it does impact how we act and react to certain situations in our lives. My theory was that as I began to feel better my ego began to make its way back in. I liked looking good and I started to have great success with my business. Though not egotistical in my day to day actions, my ego did subtly start to attach itself to the image I wanted to portray.

To summarize what I have previously written, in the fall of the year 2015 I started to attend church on a regular basis. It was called The House Church. After my divorce in 2002 we sold our family home. This was the house where I first had the experience of seeing and feeling the millions and millions of souls being so desperate to be released from a place of captivity and pass through the newly opened passage way. I believe this gateway to be an improved version of the Body of Christ. We are being called to come together and fulfill God's plan to come together in this manner.

The fellow that bought our home, Jim, was a retired civil engineer, as stated in Chapter 1. He wanted to know more about the home from the guy who built it, that being me. I of course agreed to meet. We got along very well. I felt so comfortable that the next time I went out of town I asked if my dog could stay in the pen that I had built in the back yard. The rest is history. He, my dog, and I became the best of friends.

Jim is an exemplary Christian. On most all of our many hikes, we would talk often about engineering, of course, but most importantly we would talk about God. He never judged anything that I told him about my healing and about my experiences with God, as nontraditional as they may seem to some. It was in Jim's home, my previous family home, that he started The House Church in 2015, along with a pastor who was a friend of his.

As I have described in the Introduction and in Chapter 1, from the beginning I wanted to share with the pastor all about the experiences that I had right there in the very same house where we now held our services at. I hoped he would understand why I felt so driven to speak the way I do about God and what I believe to be our role in God's plan to transform ourselves and then our planet. I wanted to tell him about the many, many souls that need to be released from captivity and thereby being delivered back to the source, to God Himself. I knew there were millions, even more, but I wanted a number to give to the pastor, and to myself, as it had been over 16 years since that experience had occurred. I felt that if I was going to be able to hear from God, through my spirit, as before, that in part, I needed to somehow minimize my ego. Humbly, now on my knees before God as I write this, I was able to find a way. Prior to relating the rest of this most profound journey, I want to first go back and continue with what I had learned and how I put it into practice.

Chapter Four

Putting What I Learned Into Practice

Recall Lesson 1, Following Your Heart. It was within the first few months of moving out of our home that I decided I also needed a career change. I worked with a great local contractor in construction management, a field I had worked in for most all of my career at that time. I was restless in my work and did not know what I wanted to do different, but I did know *what I did not want to do.* What I did not want to do was what I was doing. I remember thinking, *If you are going to talk the talk you had better be able to walk the walk.*

I had shared with many about how important our word is and our trust in God and his plan for us. Equally important was to then act on that plan. We can learn to do so by listening to that quiet, yet consistent voice inside of us. I recall sitting at my desk and upon having these thoughts I got up and walked into the office of the owner of the company. I asked if he had a minute to talk.

He said, "Yes."

I then sat down and told him that I was giving him six-months' notice. He was and is a great person and knew what I was going through.

"What are you going to do to make a living?" he asked.

At the time I was making payments for my car, my wife's car, our mortgage, my apartment rent, all of our insurance, and other expenses. She did not work.

I replied, "I don't know, but I do know that I need to make a change."

I had worked in construction management since I graduated from college, participating in the building of bridges, high rise buildings, and subways all across America. We had moved to Sedona, Arizona to escape the hectic life of the big city. When I had the experience of millions and millions of souls passing through a part of my body, I knew I must take whatever steps it took to fulfill that reality. This included the risks of not following the doctor's advice when it came to the cancer. It was my heart's desire, driven by my spirit in union with God, to make this happen.

As far as feeling the souls pass through me as previously described, it is important to note that

I now understand that our bodies are pieces of the Body of Christ.

Paul wrote in **Ephesians 5:30 NLT.**

"For we are members of His body."
1 Corinthians 12:11-12 NLT. *"All these are the work of one and the same Spirit, who apportions them to each one as He determines. The body is a unit, though it is comprised of many parts. And although its parts are many, they all form one body. So, it is with Christ."*

Thus, I take no credit, but I do simply relate what I felt, that being the souls passing through my being, a part of the Body of Christ.

What is so interesting is that a short time after I had given notice to my boss, I received a structural engineering magazine in the mail, one I did not recall ordering. I looked at the cover and it had a computer-generated image on it of what the motion of a tall, steel building would look like during an earthquake, swaying from side to side. I felt in my heart, "Yes, I would like to design something like that!" But my mind then jumped in and said, "But after you graduated you chose to build things, not design them. Your time to learn that is over." I had done quite well in school some twenty plus years earlier. I had graduated at or near the top of my class, but I was rusty at what I had learned, other than simple designs for temporary supports during the construction process. I had not learned the engineering skills needed to work on the design of high-rise buildings.

However, shortly after giving my notice, I got the phone call from the friend I previously mentioned that I had worked for in the San Francisco Bay Area. Jay was a contractor and had come up with a completely new approach to steel building construction by using concrete filled tube steel along with a to be patented quick connection. He needed someone to head up the testing and wanted to know if I was interested. Meeting specific design requirements was necessary, as then it could be approved by the building code officials. At first, he said the testing would likely take place at the structural engineering laboratory at the University of California at Berkeley. I said yes, but what was interesting was that the testing would not start until after my six months' notice that I had given to my current employer.

I then started doing some research on line and after calling around to various institutions it was recommended that I contact a professor at the University of Arizona in Tucson, Arizona. I did and he was interested. I told my friend Jay and shortly thereafter he and another engineer, a PhD, flew into the Phoenix airport. I picked them up and we drove to Tucson. The professor had us meet him in the computer laboratory. He had a few of his graduate students there and after a brief introduction he had his students turn on their computers. I was amazed by what I saw. On their screens were images very similar to what I had seen on the magazine some six months earlier!

Back when I had seen the magazine my heart had yearned to work on the design of how high-rise buildings would respond in an earthquake. And right before my eyes were images of just that! Developing similar images for our system was part of the testing procedures that would be required to get our new system approved by FEMA, the governing authority.

For the next two years we performed several tests at the engineering laboratory at the University of Arizona. The structural steel connection ultimately passed all of the testing requirements. What is also interesting was that during the process there was an ongoing disagreement between Jay, the professor, and the other PhD engineer that accompanied us on our first visit. The dispute was about how the forces reacted at the steel connection. I listened intently to both sides of the argument. Having not been in school for quite some time I wanted to agree with the professor and the other PhD, but instinct told me Jay was right. I thought about it and then wrote a four-page paper supporting Jay's design. My persistence paid off. In the end, after arguing it again and again, each time ending in disagreement, the professor looked up at the ceiling. I am sure he was envisioning the forces in the connection at work.

He then said, "Yes, I see it now, you are right."

Whatever doubt had existed in my engineering skills from not having practiced prior to starting this project, were now gone. I also had worked at the level that is needed to design the connections of high-rise buildings during an earthquake, just as my heart so very much wanted.

Shortly thereafter, I started my own engineering business in Sedona, Arizona and continue it to this date. Though very few buildings in our small town require such sophistication as that of the steel connection that we developed at the University of Arizona, all projects go through the thorough thought process that engineers put into their designs. In this story please see that my heart, as guided by my spirit that is in union with God, wanted me to fulfill who I wanted to be, and to do so I had to further my engineering abilities. It took the courage to step into my boss's office and tell him I was giving him notice and to trust in God in order to achieve the rest!

I now look back to a time prior to the illness when I had taken on a small engineering job on the side. The job site was over a two-hour drive away. While returning home I was driving down the freeway from Flagstaff while thinking about the job, when I had an epiphany. I had the most profound feeling that I indeed was a practicing engineer and had my own private business. That knowing was no coincidence and was in fact an insight of what was to come, as I have had my own engineering practice for almost twenty years now, as of the writing of this book. A most rewarding experience.

The Learning

Recall that in Ephesians Paul wrote:

> **Ephesians 4:11 NLT.** *"Now these are the gifts Christ gave to the church: the apostles, the prophets, the evangelists and the pastors and teachers. Their responsibility is to equip God's people to do his work and build up the church, the body of Christ. This will continue until we all come to such unity in our faith and knowledge of God's son that we will be mature in the Lord, measuring up to the full and complete standards of Christ."*

To me, this is one of the most powerful phrases in the Bible! Read the last part again, *"measuring up to the full and complete standards of Christ!"* Think about it! What are the standards of Christ?

Jesus made it perfectly clear when he told his Apostles in **Matthew 10:8**:

> **Matthew 10:8 NLT.** *"... heal the sick, raise the dead, cure those with leprosy, and cast out demons."*

> And in **Luke 9:1** Luke wrote, *"One day Jesus called together his twelve disciples and gave them power and authority to cast out all demons and to heal all diseases."*

> And from **Luke 10:17-20 NLT.** *"When the seventy-two disciples returned, they joyfully reported to him, "Lord, even the demons obey us when we use your name!"*

> > *"Yes," he told them. "I saw Satan fall from Heaven like lightening! Look, I have given you authority over all the power of the enemy, and you can walk among snakes and scorpions and crush them. Nothing will injure you. But don't rejoice because evil spirits obey you: rejoice because your names are registered in heaven."*

From the above we learn what the *"full and complete standards of Christ"* are. It is also clear that as we begin to achieve these standards step-by-step we rejoice not because of our deeds, but because we are humble and reverent to God. In Romans Paul wrote:

> **Romans 8:29-30 NLT.** *"For God knew his people in advance, and he chose them to become like his Son, so that his Son would be the first born among many brothers and sisters."*

Here again it is clear that we are to become like Christ. This is a big task. How do we come to better our ability to do this?

In Romans 8:26 Paul wrote,

> **Romans 8:26 NLT.** *"And the Holy Spirit helps us in our weakness."*

I can only speak for myself but God certainly knows my shortcomings. He also knows that we cannot become more like Christ until we work towards overcoming these weaknesses. From my healing in the year 2002 when I heard through my spirit that, "The reason for my illness was now over" until now, the areas which I needed to improve myself have been made clear, one by one. They have included overcoming my insecurities, and realizing and improving upon any personality glitches.

One thing that I had to learn was the power of self-expression. God gave us a voice, a mind, a right brain for creativity, and a left brain for math and science. I was doing well with the use of my left brain, but not so much with the use of my right brain. Then, in the year 2003 my cousin asked me to attend an event held in the desert where many people gathered to show their various forms of art. I attended this event and was blown away by the amount of self-expression, either in painting, sculptures, dance, or music, and more.

When I got home, I bought some paints, an easel, and some canvas. Within a few months I produced a dozen paintings or so. I then took singing lessons and soon started writing and singing my own songs. I was amazed at how when given the opportunity to perform in public a time or two, I did so with little intimidation, as I had never sung before, let alone in public. It was because of the health challenges that I had overcome, and because of wanting to leave no stone unturned in my search for my calling, that I was able to perform so easily in public. Within a couple of years, I had written and recorded about thirty songs which included a rock opera. What was equally amazing was that I found the professionals to help me do so right in Sedona, with a nice recording studio not far from my home.

I then ran for public office as an Independent for a seat in the U.S. Congress. I did not win, as it is tough for an unknown candidate to do so, but the experience once again was one of personal growth. As an engineer we tell people what to do and they do it. As a candidate running for public office the voters expect the opposite, they want you to do and say what they want. They want to know who you are on the inside, not what you present on the outside as your profession.

I would get questions like, "What do you think about abortion?" and, "How do you feel about gay marriage?" These, of course, had nothing to do with how good of an engineer I was.

For me, I needed all these experiences. It was important that I express myself in ways I had never done before. I learned to do so without worrying what people thought and just did so knowing that it was coming from my soul and heart. All of this was very rewarding. This was especially true when a couple of years ago I acted in a play for the very first time. I had a key role, playing the Apostle Thomas, where I had to act and sing a solo. This in itself was perhaps the most rewarding experience of them all, not only from the acting, but because of the joy it brought me. Even my spirit sang out in a state of bliss!

I recall being at one of the final rehearsals. I had finally learned all my lines, knew my positions on stage, and was doing well with the rhythm of the songs. This took a lot of work, something I practiced at every day. I was so happy that I ran and then slid across the stage in stocking feet, at least I think I had on socks but no shoes, otherwise I do not know how I could have slid so effortlessly across the stage. But there was never a reason to take off our shoes. I don't know. Anyway, as I came to the end of my slide, I remember thinking to myself, *Wow, that was really cool.* I was singing my lines as I was sliding on the stage! Then I realized, hey, I don't have any lines at this scene, neither speaking nor singing! I realized that it was my spirit that was singing inside of me. It was singing with such joy!

That evening I went home and lay upon the couch. I thought of what had taken place within my spirit, soul and physical body! I then said to God, what about the one billion souls? I was then rewarded with three souls passing through my being! Swoosh, swoosh, swoosh they went as I felt them pass through. This joyful experience we will discuss later more in detail, but it led me to believe that likely these were the souls of the dead, not the living.

Self-expression and the ability to do it well is absolute key in doing God's work for him. We must be confident, competent, and be able to deliver our message in a very natural way, to be who God made us to be, and complete the job he sent us to do.

Not all of the growth, however, was fun, as this work of self-improvement also took place in my relationships with women. No need to go into the details. But needless to say, a break-up and a heart that has been hurt can lead to a lot of challenges, and when handled properly, a lot of self- improvement. This includes the ending of an unhealthy relationship when it's time to do so. This, God knew, I was not good at, at least not for a few years. I am now in a healthy relationship, and guess who with? The lady at my surprise birthday party that saw the Holy Spirit blow out the candles. It is interesting how God works.

Recently, I was challenged in my work which was the most protected part of my personality. When we do our work well that is good, but we also tend to then take that and create a shield around us, one that we think protects us. We don't want anyone to see us on the inside, who we truly are, our hurts, or our pain. So, we then project outwards what we want them to see. This particular lesson had to do with a project I had worked on. The neighbor was really upset as the new house I had engineered blocked a wonderful view that they had enjoyed for about twenty years. They had a relative that was an engineer look over the plans and my calculations. When I got a copy of the complaint from the governing jurisdiction I just about had a heart attack, well, not really, but it was quite upsetting. My outer shell had been broken and the fear of having really screwed up became my reality, at least for a short while.

The complaint was lengthy and it took several hours to go through it line by line. To my relief, I realized that the engineer was not trained in my discipline and had made several mistakes in her assessment. My lesson was that the shell I had placed around me for so many years of being competent in the work performed and in the presentation of myself to my clients had been broken, at least temporarily. Before having taken time to study the document I had such a terrible feeling, one of exposure and fear.

The good news was I did take the opportunity to address those fears. Soon after I got the notice, I was lying awake at night, thinking of what had happened. That is when I felt the fear. At first it seemed to encompass me. However, I recognized what was happening, that is losing myself to the fear. I then set aside any thoughts of how to resolve damages the situation might have on the project and on my reputation. I literally called on the fear itself and looked directly at it, face to face. Remember, everything is energy, including fear. I then put the thought of unconditional love, or agape love as described in Lessons 2, 8, and 9, onto it. Within a few moments it was gone, and after doing this for only two nights it never came back.

I had successfully dealt with the fear, that which came up from my inner most self. After doing so I was then able to come up with solutions to the issues brought up. It wasn't long after that that I realized that all the complaints were grossly inaccurate! I wrote a five page report and disproved each and every claim. By the time I submitted this document to the governing authorities, not only had I cleared up any and all issues having to do with the fear, but I came out an even stronger person. That fear had been uncovered and eliminated from my being. So, in this respect, the overall experience was for the good.

We Are Becoming Priests

1 Peter 2:5 NLT. *"And you are living stones that God is building into his spiritual temple. What's more, you are his holy priests..."*

Revelations 5: 9-10 NLT. *"You are worthy to take the scroll and break its seals and open it. For you were slaughtered, and your blood has ransomed people for God from every tribe and language and people and nation. And you have caused them to become a Kingdom of priests for our God. And they will reign on the earth."*

I recall soon after I bought my first Bible in the fall of 2016 I woke with a message from my spirit, in union with God of course. The message said 1 Peter 2:5. Not having ever read the Bible I had no idea what this message from spirit meant. I got up from bed, went into my office where my Bible was kept and read from 1 Peter 2:5. Having this message come through the way it did make an impression on me, as I believe it would for anyone. Based on this, and on the spiritual experiences that I have written about, there is no doubt that we all are indeed destined to become priests. Recall, Christ was a priest, and we are to become a Christ.

> **Ephesians 4:11-13 NLT.** *"Now these are the gifts Christ gave to the church: the apostles, the prophets, the evangelists, and the pastors and teachers. Their responsibility is to equip God's people to do his work and build up the church, the body of Christ. This will continue until we all come to such unity in our faith and knowledge of God's Son that we will be mature in the Lord, measuring up to the full and complete standard of Christ."*

It is not only our duty but the desire of our souls and spirits to seek God, to act on his behalf and to do all we can to meet his standards.

Roman 8:29 NLT. *"For God knew his people in advance, so that his Son would be the firstborn among many brothers and sisters. And having chosen them, he called them to come to him. And having called them, he gave them right standing with himself. And having right standing, he gave them glory."*

This is God's calling and this is the time to answer and become the representative of God by becoming the priests that we are meant to be. To do so we must become our true selves.

Free to Be Me

We know we are getting closer to becoming who we are meant to be when we feel joy in our hearts. I recall two of my friends counting all of their steps by using the step app on their cell phones. It was to the point where they seemed obsessed with it. I thought it was kind of silly but because I loved them so much these little idiosyncrasies had no significance. A few months later one of them challenged us to a friendly fitness competition which included keeping track of our daily steps. I too then began counting my steps. One evening I was at 14,000 steps. Before reporting in I wanted to hit 15,000. I was over at my lady Barbara's house. While she was getting ready for the evening, I started walking around her living room. It took

25 steps for one lap. All I had to do was forty laps and I could reach my goal of 15,000 steps.

By the time Barb came back into the room I had done over thirty laps. What was interesting was that I was having a great time in doing so! It was really fun. It was also freeing, as it was perfectly fine with Barb. She even joined me for a few laps. It's what I now call "Free to Be Me." I was being myself. I was having fun competing with my friends, both of which lived in a different state. Most significantly I could simply be myself around Barb and in her home. This is very important. We cannot be who God made us to be, we cannot all become priests, if we are not free within ourselves to do so. Being in a great relationship where you are free to be yourself is an important step in doing so.

A Letter to the Pope

In the fall of 2018, Barbara and I traveled to Italy with my two friends, Andy and OJ, that I was having the step competition with, along with their wives. At this point I had told only a select few about my revelation of participating in the freeing one billion souls. I had told Barbara and she was very receptive. I had also told both of my friends, as they have been two of my best friends since high school. In Rome we visited the Vatican. While there the idea came to me that I needed to write a letter to the Pope and tell him of the one billion souls. That night I woke early, perhaps 4:00 AM. Fortuitously, I had been purifying my mind and therefore my body for several weeks. While lying there I started thinking of what I wanted to say in my letter. Just the thought of the one billion souls and imagining writing about them to the Pope certainly got my spirit activated. It was then that I tapped into the essence of the Pope. His soul was quite pure. Let's say if he was at 100 out of 100, I was at about a 96.

The next thing I saw was a very black tornado spinning around. This whirling mass of dark energy was certainly from within the Vatican itself and was of the devil, but I do not believe it came from the Pope himself. The darkness that I found makes sense as it was not long before our trip to Italy that while again watching EWTN they reported that the Vatican Police had broken up a gay sex party taking place right inside the Vatican. Even more disturbing was that the priest involved, a 49-year-old Monsignor Luigi Capozzi, was the secretary to a Cardinal Francesco Coccopalmerio. Coccopalmerio was one of the advisors to the Pope. Equally disturbing was that male homosexuals from Rome were involved.

In addition to the news about the gay sex party, Raymond Arroyo, commentator on the Catholic TV station EWTN, did an entire show in 2018 on an eleven-page letter written by Archbishop Vigano. In this document Vigano claimed that the Pope and other Vatican officials were covering up sex abuse in the church. Also, according to Dr. Taylor Marshall, a Catholic author, during the time of Pope Benedict XVI Vigano was appointed by Pope Benedict to the position of Secretary-General of the Governorate of the Vatican City. Accordingly, Vigano knew what was going on in the Vatican quite well. Furthermore, in 2012 Pope Benedict appointed three of his most trusted cardinals to investigate the scandal of the IOR, known as the Vatican Bank. Marshall then goes on to state that these three cardinals subsequently wrote a 300-page report for Pope Benedict. In it they stated that the IOR was not only corrupt but those in charge were reported to have several homosexual encounters.

The Arroyo report on the gay sex party to the Vatican Bank scandal confirmed the darkness that I saw when I tapped into the energy of the Vatican. Realize that a tornado sucks up anything and everything that is not very securely attached to its foundation. Unfortunately, many within the ranks of those in the Vatican have been swept away by this darkness. In a later chapter I write about how to close the devil's door. This is something that those consumed by this tornado of darkness need to learn how to do, as the devil is behind all the troubles within the Vatican.

Knowing how Satan works is helpful when it comes to better understanding what has happened inside of the Vatican, and in the rest of the world.

In Chapter 6 I discuss how I watched a program on spiritual warfare. The priest giving the presentation was a Father Ripperger of the Roman Catholic Church. His knowledge of how the devil works is second to none. In particular he speaks of Satan's top four generals, giving their names and their particular specialty of evil. One of these demon's specialty is homosexuality. There is no doubt in my mind that the Roman Catholic Church itself could use Father Ripperger's expertise.

The devil has made his way into the hierarchy of the Roman Catholic Church and it appears that the Pope has not handled it correctly. However, I do not believe that Pope Francis is corrupt, as the energy of his soul was too pure to be so. We also do not know how difficult it must be to try and clean up such a mess. Either way, this problem must be resolved or God will do it for us, and that will not be a pretty site. See The Dream of the Comet in a subsequent chapter.

After having the experience of tapping into the purity of the Pope's soul, and then witnessing the dark tornado from within the Vatican, I got up and started writing my letter. Interestingly enough I was able to do it on my phone and then email it to the front desk of our hotel and have them print it for me in the morning. In the letter I introduced myself. I gave a brief history of the miraculous healing that I had had and that I was the Architect and Engineer for the San Francisco de Asis Roman Catholic Church and School in Flagstaff, Arizona. I also mentioned the other engineering projects I was doing for the church. I then gave details of the one billion souls and how I had come about this revelation. The next day Barbara and I took a taxi over to the Vatican and mailed the letter in the Vatican postal box. Writing this letter was a big deal for me.

The Pope never did write back, for whatever reason, perhaps it never made it to his desk. But that does not matter as when I came back to the states, I found that I was telling far more people than ever before about the one billion souls. I told how they are so desperate to get out from where they are and be able to go to what I will call home. I am sure this strong desire is to be in unity with God and of course with Christ. Quite likely this is in Heaven.

It was two or three months after this that I was wondering what I could do next to pursue this calling that I felt so deeply. A friend had just finished up a radio show that he was doing for a book that he had written. It was then that I thought of starting my own radio show and that

I would base it on the draft of this book that I had written at that time. I asked a very learned and wise friend, Bart Chapman, to be my co-host. After tossing around a few possibilities for the name of the show I decided on calling it The Freeing of One Billion Souls. Having written to the Pope about the one billion souls actually freed me up. By the time we debuted our show on 1100 KFNX out of Phoenix, Arizona in May of 2019 we were telling many thousands. This experience in its self was next to none. If you want to express yourself from the very deepest place in your soul and your spirit, doing it on radio is a great place to start.

There is no doubt in my mind that all of the life experiences and opportunities for self-expression since my miraculous healing were absolutely essential in preparing me to better do God's work, to become more like His son. This continued with the radio show. The first several shows covered topics written about in this book, as stated. In particular, we discussed the 9 lessons and then continued our topics related to God from there. Bart did an excellent job in asking questions from statements I made both on air and from within my book. We aired over thirty times from early May 2019 until December 31, 2019. All of this freedom to speak out about such an important subject came about as a result of taking the initiative to write a letter to the Pope. "After all," I had thought, "if I can tell the Pope I can tell anyone!"

Saint Teresa of Avila

In the winter of 2018, after returning from our trip to Europe when I had written a letter to Pope Francis, I was lying awake in bed. I felt compelled to not only purify my own mind, soul and body, but also that part of the Body of Christ that had been so stained by the darkness from within the Catholic Church, as previously described. I recall thinking, *How could I be so arrogant as to think that I could purify the Body of Christ?*

I then went back to that space in my mind that felt so natural and guided by my spirit, the very same place that got me through my illness some eighteen years earlier. I have learned to focus on and pursue the energetic pattern that I felt. What I knew was that not only was I purifying my own body, but that of a portion of the Body of Christ, as well. Accordingly, I continued to do just that. Sometime after I fell asleep, I awoke to the presence of Saint Teresa of Avila. When these things happen, it is typically not a visual I get, but a very clear spiritual knowing. I am so confident in these experiences as it is the energetic form that I feel and am totally aware of. After all, she has a spiritual body, not a physical body. I was baffled as to why she made an appearance, as there was no message given. So, I went back to sleep.

The next day Barb and I left for our road trip to Los Angeles to see her son. While driving we were listening to a set of three CD's that we had purchased through EWTN. The speaker was a Catholic apologist who, by the way, had previously been a Protestant apologist. One of the three CD's was about the reformation started by Martin Luther. The speaker went on to say that because of the corruption within the Catholic Church, Saint Teresa of Avila, a Christian Mystic, wrote that she was compelled to purify the church through her mystical meditation and purification process. This is exactly what I had done the night before. Once again, a spiritual experience that I had was confirmed. Confirmation such as this is always important. We must take the initiative to be who God made us to be!

An Experience with Shamanism

In Chapter 3 I wrote how I came to know the distinction between the soul and the spirit. I expand on this further in Chapter 7. However, while still going through the healing process I heard a fellow speak while I was attending a conference in Palm Springs, California. This was before I started to read the Bible. This individual, whose name I am intentionally leaving out, was giving a talk on shamanism. What caught my attention was that this particular individual spoke on what he called the three levels of the soul. His description was in complete alignment with what I have come know. That being the soul is comprised of the emotions and a portion of the mind. The only difference was he called the spirit the "over-soul".

I was quite curious as to how this fellow had come across this information, as up until then I had not heard anyone else speak on it. Accordingly, I attended a couple of his work shops. This teacher knew his subject matter well, and always used love when explaining how to journey into the spirit world. He also spoke on how shamanic methods can be used for the good for healing, but that some also use it for ill intent. This I already knew, as too often shamanic practices in South America include placing negative energies into others, including the use of what I call psychic daggers.

What I did come to know was that this teacher knew nothing of the interdimensional world and, more importantly, nothing of Christ. Therefore he knew nothing about the Body of Christ and how we are all to become Christ like ourselves. Remember Ephesians 4 from the New Testament.

> **Ephesians 4: 13 NLT**, "*This will continue until we all come to such unity in our faith and knowledge of God's Son that we will be mature in the Lord,*

measuring up to the full and complete standard of Christ."

Chapter Five

The Battle in the Heavenly Realms

After the first 20 shows or so of our radio show Bart and I had covered all 9 lessons of my book. I recall asking God, "What next?" as we thought we had run out of topics. I went for a walk, as this is when I do my most effective problem solving. Taking a break and walking clears the mind. The next thing I knew in my spirit I was involved in a great battle. I was surrounded by hoards and hoards of the enemy, thousands and thousands, perhaps as many as ten thousand! Imagine yourself being right in the middle of one of the great battles of ancient times when they used swords, shields, and arrows as weapons. Yet, in this battle they could not touch me and therefore paid no attention to me! This was apparently because I had my armor on. Saint Paul wrote in Ephesians:

> **Ephesians 6:13-19 NLT.** *"Therefore, put on every piece of Gods armor so you will be able to resist the enemy in the time of evil. Then after the battle you will still be standing firm. Stand your ground, putting on the belt of truth and*

*the body armor of God's righteousness.
For shoes put on the peace that comes
from the Good News so that you will be
fully prepared. In addition to all of these
hold up the shield of faith to stop the
fiery arrows of the devil. Put on
salvation as your helmet, and take the
sword of the Spirit, which is the word of
God."*

Having had this experience with being amongst
so many of the enemy I knew this was a topic
that we had to discuss on the show. A client had
recently given me a title of a book by a fellow
named Rick Joyner. I had never heard of him
nor, of course, had I read any of his books. The
name of the book that the client had given me
was The Torch and the Sword. I found a copy
on the Internet and began to read. It was about
the author in his spirit witnessing the great
ongoing battle in the Heavenly realms. In it he
describes how many of those he met were
indeed surrounded by hoards of the enemy.
What he wrote about was the same as I had
experienced.

What is interesting is that when in tune with our
spirit, which of course is in union with the Holy
Spirit, what we perceive as being truth here on
the Earthly realms is in fact true in the Heavenly
realms. For example, often I have felt that far
too many leaders of the various denominations
of the Christian religion are actually holding

people back from knowing God. They are often overzealous and indoctrinated, and end up limiting their members' spiritual growth. As far as bringing new people to the faith they end up chasing off more than they bring in. This is unfortunate as God is amazing! Knowing him and Christ and as a result becoming to know who you truly are and your role in the greater plan is powerful, rewarding, and joyful! This does not come from the teachings of a self-absorbed Bible shaking preacher.

I once met a minister who while talking to me pointed to his diploma on the wall, as if that gave him some sort of authority. I understand the importance of education, as an engineer I needed a diploma to graduate. But knowing God comes first from and through the spirit, not the intellect. Knowing the Bible is important, but limiting the spiritual aspect is potentially dangerous. If a preacher falls into the aforementioned scenario, he is in fact helping the enemy.

It is important to note that we do not want to harshly criticize fellow Christians, but we do need to discern what a healthy form of Christianity is. If we are not doing our best to emit agape love to those we strongly disagree with, while we are expressing our opinion, we then are not helping the cause. This is especially true if we feel superior to others while doing so. Also, harshly criticizing a member of the Body of Christ is harshly criticizing a part of you, which is not a good idea! But again, we do need to be discerning. Recall Saint Paul, when he was known as Saul, when approached by Christ while on the road to Damascus.

Christ said, "Why are you persecuting me?"

By "me" he meant those individuals whom Saul had indeed persecuted, who were members of the Body of Christ. So, when I make statements about various preachers whom I strongly disagree with in their methods, I do my best to be accurate and with as much understanding and hopefully with as much agape love that I can give. This is important.

In the battle in the Heavenly realms, if we shoot arrows of truth at those blindfolded Christians who, as Joyner describes, are being ridden like horses by the enemy, it only makes them angry. The same is true here on Earth. If we speak truth to those preachers who do more harm than good it has the same result, they get mad. The key is to love them, not to criticize them, as if we are greater than they are.

In 1 Corinthians Paul wrote:

> **1 Corinthians NLT.** *"But while knowledge makes us feel important, it is love that strengthens the church. Anyone who claims to know all the answers*

doesn't really know very much. But the person whom loves God is the person whom God recognizes. "

So, we must be humble in our observations of others. Yet, we must become more aware and more discerning of what others are teaching.

An example of a good teacher, though he does not speak on the battle in the Heavenly realms to my knowledge, is Andrew Wommack, a preacher from Colorado. He has had great success in bringing people to Christ, to his explanation of the Bible and how to interpret it, and in his healing ministry. Yet, when I brought his name up to some of the local ministers, they put him down. Why? Because they are getting their toes stepped on. They become territorial and self-centered, not wanting to lose control over their flock. This is sad as it does not allow for their members to decide for themselves as to what teaching is true for them. It is also sad as it actually empowers the enemy in the battle in the Heavenly realms. In Joyner's books he tells how tens of thousands of Christians have allowed themselves to be blindfolded. They are being ridden like horses by demons and used in battle against other Christians whom have not allowed themselves to be led astray. This is not good, yet it is our reality. Go into a church and speak your truth. If the preacher perceives you as a threat to his domain and responds with anger he is being ridden like a horse. However, the battle goes on and ultimately, though heavily outnumbered, the forces of good shall prevail.

And what weapons do the demons use against us? In Ephesians Paul wrote:

> **Ephesians 6:16 NLT.** *"Hold up the shield of faith to stop the fiery arrows of the devil."*

The enemy shoots arrows of temptation, of lust, greed, depression, feeling inferior to others or arrogantly superior to others, and any insecurity that you can think of. These are the weapons of the devil. As we learn to close the devil's door, these weapons cannot penetrate our shield, but until we learn to do so we are subject to being wounded.

The battle in the Heavenly realms is just as real as the world we live in, in fact more so. As it is clear there what we are fighting for and whom we are fighting against. What we need to understand is that our actions here on Earth directly impacts that which is occurring in this battle! We make a difference here on Earth. To limit evil from making its way into our culture and our society in our Earthly realm we must put up a good fight and effectively join this battle in the Heavenly realm. We do so by gaining knowledge of God within us, and in particular, in whom God made us to be. In becoming this, we must express ourselves with our words and actions what it is that our spirit wants us to say and do. Recall, this is not a God somewhere outside of us, but it is who we truly are, it is God within us. We are his temple. It is time to be bold in who we are! In 1 John 2:28 John said:

> **1 John 2:28 NLT.** *"And now, dear children, remain in fellowship with Christ so that when he returns you will be full of courage and not shrink back from him in shame."*

In 1 Thessalonians 2:12 Paul wrote:

> **1 Thessalonians NLT.** *"We pleaded with you, encouraged you, and urged you to live your lives in a way that God would consider worthy. For he called you to share in his Kingdom and glory."*

God is indeed calling us and we cannot fulfill that call if we do not change the way we live. To fully participate in defeating evil here on Earth and in the battle in the Heavenly realms we must live a life up to the, *"...full and complete standards of Christ,"* Ephesians 4:12, to the best of our ability. This is a big calling, but it is one that cannot be ignored.

In 2 Thessalonians Paul wrote:

2 Thessalonians 1:11NLT. *"So, we keep on praying for you, asking our God to enable you to live a life worthy of his call."*

Here again we see biblically where God is indeed calling us!

In 1 Corinthians Paul wrote:

1 Corinthians 3:16 NLT. *"Don't you realize that all of you together are the temple of God and that the Spirit of God lives in you.... For God's temple is holy, and you are that temple."*

Here, Paul is speaking of the Body of Christ as he says, *"all of you together are the temple"*, but as the Spirit of God lives in all of us collectively, it lives in each of us individually. We represent God here on Earth, so make yourself worthy of such a cause.

It is important that we have faith and endurance when answering this call. From James:

James 1:2-8 NLT. *"Dear brothers and sisters, when troubles of any kind come your way, consider it an opportunity for great joy. For you know that when your faith is tested, your endurance has a chance to grow. So, let it grow, for when your endurance is fully developed,* *you will be perfect and complete, needing nothing.*

If you need wisdom, ask our generous God, and he will give it to you. He will not rebuke you for asking. But when you ask him, be sure that your faith is in God alone. Do not waver, for a person with divided loyalty is as unsettled as a wave of the sea that is blown and tossed by the wind. Such people should not expect to receive anything from the Lord. Their loyalty is divided between God and the world, and they are unstable in everything they do."

And in **12-18** James wrote,

"God blesses those who patiently endure testing and temptation. Afterward they will receive the crown of life that God has promised to those who love him. And remember, when you are being tempted, do not say, "God is tempting me." God is never tempted to do wrong, and he never tempts anyone else. Temptation comes from our own desires, which entice us and drag us away. These desires give birth to sinful actions. And when sin is allowed to grow, it gives birth to death.

So, don't be misled, my dear brothers and sisters. Whatever is good and perfect is a gift coming down to us from God our Father, who created all the lights in the heavens. He never changes or casts a shifting shadow. He chose to give birth to us by giving us his true word. And we, out of all creation, became his prized possession."

Here, we are given insight into how to lead a life away from temptation. Remember the importance of lesson 7, the Purification of Thought.

To best fight the battle, we must do the work. As it is written in James:

> **James 2:14 NLT.** *"Faith without Good Deeds is Dead."*

I get frustrated when various preachers pound in faith and disregard works. Faith and works go hand in hand. Disregarding the significance of works is misguided indoctrination that has been around since the reformation. It is time, my brothers and sisters, to be discerning about what you are being taught. To be clear, I am not diminishing the importance of faith, for without it we have nothing. But I am emphasizing the importance of doing the work.

Faith Without Good Deeds Is Dead

The Apostle James so eloquently wrote in the following:

James 2 NLT. Faith without Good Deeds Is Dead

"What good is it, dear brothers and sisters, if you say you have faith but don't show it by your actions? Can that kind of faith save anyone? Suppose you see a brother or sister who has no food or clothing, and you say, "Good-bye and have a good day; stay warm and eat well"—but then you don't give that person any food or clothing. What good does that do?

So, you see, faith by itself isn't enough. Unless it produces good deeds, it is dead and useless.

Now someone may argue, "Some people have faith; others have good deeds."

But I say, "How can you show me your faith if you don't have good deeds? I will show you my faith by my good deeds."

You say you have faith, for you believe that there is one God. Good for you! Even the demons believe this, and they tremble in terror. How foolish! Can't you see that faith without good deeds is useless?

Don't you remember that our ancestor Abraham was shown to be right with God by his actions when he offered his son Isaac on the altar? You see, his faith and his actions worked together. His actions made his faith complete."

James 2:23-25 NLT. *"And so, it happened just as the Scriptures say "Abraham believed God, and God counted him as righteous because of his faith." He was even called the friend of God. So, you see, we are shown to be right with God by what we do, not by faith alone.*

Rahab the prostitute is another example. She was shown to be right with God by her actions when she hid those messengers and sent them safely away by a different road."

James 2:26 NLT. *"Just as the body is dead without breath, so also faith is dead without good works."*

Need I say more when the apostle James has said it so well?

The book of James gives further insight into knowing how to better do our part in living a better life, which in turn allows for us to better participate in the ongoing battle in the Heavenly realms. In **James 4** James wrote:

Drawing Close to God

> *"What is causing the quarrels and fights among you? Don't they come from the evil desires at war within you? You want what you don't have, so you scheme and kill to get it. You are jealous of what others have, but you can't get it, so you fight and wage war to take it away from them. Yet you don't have what you want because you don't ask God for it. And even when you ask, you don't get it because your motives are all wrong—you want only what will give you pleasure.*

> *You adulterers! Don't you realize that friendship with the world makes you an enemy of God? I say it again: If you want to be a friend of the world, you make yourself an enemy of God. Do you think the Scriptures have no meaning? They say that God is passionate that the spirit he has placed within us should be*

faithful to him. And he gives grace generously. As the Scriptures say,

"God opposes the proud but gives grace to the humble."

So humble yourselves before God. Resist the devil, and he will flee from you. Come close to God, and God will come close to you. Wash your hands, you sinners; purify your hearts, for your loyalty is divided between God and the world. Let there be tears for what you have done. Let there be sorrow and deep grief. Let there be sadness instead of laughter, and gloom instead of joy. Humble yourselves before the Lord, and he will lift you up in honor."

Warning against Judging Others

"Don't speak evil against each other, dear brothers and sisters. If you criticize and judge each other, then you are criticizing and judging God's law. But your job is to obey the law, not to judge whether it applies to you. God alone, who gave the law, is the Judge. He alone has the power to save or to destroy. So, what right do you have to judge your neighbor?"

Warning about Self-Confidence

"Look here, you who say, "Today or tomorrow we are going to a certain town and will stay there a year. We will do business there and make a profit." How do you know what your life will be like tomorrow? Your life is like the morning fog—it's here a little while, then it's gone. What you ought to say is, "If the Lord wants us to, we will live and do this or that." Otherwise you are boasting about your own pretentious plans, and all such boasting is evil.

Remember, it is sin to know what you ought to do and then not do it."

And from **James 5:**

Warning to the Rich

"Look here, you rich people: Weep and groan with anguish because of all the terrible troubles ahead of you. Your wealth is rotting away, and your fine clothes are moth-eaten rags. Your gold and silver are corroded. The very wealth you were counting on will eat away your flesh like fire. This corroded treasure you have hoarded will testify against you on the day of judgment. For listen! Hear the cries of the field workers whom you

have cheated of their pay. The cries of those who harvest your fields have reached the ears of the Lord of Heaven's Armies.

You have spent your years on earth in luxury, satisfying your every desire. You have fattened yourselves for the day of slaughter. You have condemned and killed innocent people, who do not resist you."

Patience and Endurance

"Dear brothers and sisters, be patient as you wait for the Lord's return. Consider the farmers who patiently wait for the rains in the fall and in the spring. They eagerly look for the valuable harvest to ripen. You, too, must be patient. Take courage, for the coming of the Lord is near.

Don't grumble about each other, brothers and sisters, or you will be judged. For look—the Judge is standing at the door!

For examples of patience in suffering, dear brothers and sisters, look at the prophets who spoke in the name of the Lord. We give great honor to those who endure under suffering. For instance,

*you know about Job, a man of great
endurance. You can see how the Lord
was kind to him at the end, for the Lord
is full of tenderness and mercy.*

*But most of all, my brothers and sisters,
never take an oath, by heaven or earth
or anything else. Just say a simple yes or
no, so that you will not sin and be
condemned."*

The Power of Prayer

*"Are any of you suffering hardships?
You should pray. Are any of you happy?
You should sing praises. Are any of you
sick? You should call for the elders of
the church to come and pray over you,
anointing you with oil in the name of the
Lord. Such a prayer offered in faith will
heal the sick, and the Lord will make you
well. And if you have committed any
sins, you will be forgiven.*

*Confess your sins to each other and pray
for each other so that you may be
healed. The earnest prayer of a
righteous person has great power and
produces wonderful results. Elijah was
as human as we are, and yet when he
prayed earnestly that no rain would fall,
none fell for three and a half years!
Then, when he prayed again, the sky sent*

down rain and the earth began to yield its crops."

Restore Wandering Believers

> *"My dear brothers and sisters, if someone among you wanders away from the truth and is brought back, you can be sure that whoever brings the sinner back from wandering will save that person from death and bring about the forgiveness of many sins.*"

All of the above scriptures from the book of James give sound advice on how we are to participate in the battle in the Heavenly realms. Whether or not we are consciously aware of this battle, by living a better life we will help the forces of good over evil both in the Heavenly realms and here on Earth.

Chapter Six

Dreams and their significance

Our dreams are a method by which our spirit, in union with God's spirit, can communicate with us. However, most of our dreams are, of course, not God talking to us. So, like all things, we must be discerning. I have had several powerful dreams and spiritual experiences over the past thirty years. Many are not relevant to my message; thus, I have not included them.

In January of 2018 I attended a three-day event where Andrew Wommack was speaking. Within a short while I had one of the dreams described in this chapter, the Cleansing of Fire. Wommack did not speak directly on this subject. However, being in an atmosphere where truth of Christ and the Bible is accurately expressed will influence the subconscious mind. Though I do not agree with everything he says, it was a pleasure to hear a preacher like Andrew Wommack speak. His message was in alignment with my own experiences and subsequent understanding about who God is and who we truly are. As stated in Luke 9:1, we do have the authority to heal the sick and cast out the demons. Considering that all of the experiences described in lessons 1 through 9 were without me going to church or even owning a Bible, it was nice to have such a knowledgeable preacher reinforce those experiences through Biblical teachings.

The following are some of my dreams and are in the chronological order by which they were received:

Dream of the Fall

On November 14, 2016 I had a dream. It took place in my bedroom in our family home in Redding, California, the home I grew up in. Several of my friends were with me in the room. I was my current age, in my early sixties. A somewhat distraught young woman came into the room. Because I did not know her, or why she was there, I did not have much to say to her. Annoyed, she made her way further into the room amongst my friends. It was night time and all were lying down. Since she was the only female, I called to her, as I did not think it right for her to have to sleep amongst all the men. She came over to me and with an upset look in her face, went out of the room, and down the stairs. I followed her. She then went outside and was leaving the premises. I went after her and caught up with her in our front yard.

I asked, "Why are you so upset with me?"

She looked at me and said, "You do not remember!"

"Remember what?" I asked.

Even more upset; she pulled out a hand written note on a piece of paper, and gave it to me to read. On it was written how she and I knew each other long before I was born. It went on to explain that I would be going away and there would be a fall of mankind, and that I would forget all that I knew. It continued to state that she was to come and find me, as she and I were very close, likely lovers. This is why she was so upset that I did not recognize her. It also became clear that she was from the past and that where she lived there had been no fall, no separation from God. She was able to time travel to find me, now. At the bottom of the note was my signature. Having seen this, my memories started to return. I began to remember who I was before I took on the assignment to perform my duties on planet Earth.

I woke from this dream, still feeling its impact. Then I dozed off again. This time I was on Earth, but it was thousands of years ago. I was in the lobby of a very tall building. The ceiling was at least 100 feet in height. I was with two other men and a young woman. She was trying to tell one of the men something that was very important to her. Suddenly, the lights in the room went out. I looked outside and darkness had overcome the out of doors as well. I instinctively knew that the entire world had gone dark. The four of us were surprised by what had taken place.

Instinctively, I knew I had to climb upwards, to make our way out of that building. The walls of the lobby were straight up but did have adequate hand holds for experienced climbers. Acting in unison all four of us began to make our way up the wall. I then realized that the questions asked by the woman to one of the men made it clear that she was in fact a time traveler from the future. She came specifically to find this young man and to help him make it through the period of darkness that was to come. It was also apparent that she was pregnant with his child, with him from the future. In order for her to meet him in the future she had to make sure that he made it through this monumental event.

As we were climbing, over half way up, I looked down and a portion of the wall below began to move as if something was pushing on it from behind. Then it became clear that that section of wall, about fifty feet in length and twelve feet in height, was indeed a large doorway. Then, as if it had been planned, the horizontal bars that were holding the door closed came off. The entire bottom portion was a hinge and the door fell open. To my amazement I saw dozens of the most evil looking demons starting to come out, the worst of the worst. Thousands of flying black bugs were the first out. They were followed by monster looking beings with massive legs and arms with distorted faces. Several human looking ones with sinister looks on their faces were intermingled with the monsters, all stepping out together.

Immediately, I thought, *Boy, it is going to take a long, long time to collect all of these evil doers and seal them back up again.*

I then woke up.

This was my dream of the Fall of mankind. God certainly was aware of this before it took place, and he knew when he sent his messengers, they would forget who they were. So, he arranged for them to be reminded in their dreams, at least this is my take on it.

Dream of the Comet

From my diary in the year 2017. Last night I had some interesting dreams. My son Taylor and I were in Trump's entourage. We spent the night in a mid-sized house in a small town. It was two stories with a small bedroom in a third level. Trump and Melania gave up their bed on the second story for me and went up to the third floor. Sometime before or after this dream I saw a comet headed towards Earth. Fortunately, it broke up into half a dozen smaller pieces before it hit but still each piece was likely the size of a football field. I think the fact that my and others level of consciousness raising up had a lot to do with the asteroid breaking up. Accordingly, the message that the comet hitting and "knocking some sense into us" would give, did not need to be as strong (good thing). From above I saw the pieces hit, bam, bam, bam, three into the ocean on the left side of a land mass, starting at the south and headed north, one after another. The fourth moved to the right, at the top (kind of like Italy) and it hit a populated center. Then, later I had another dream. I was counseling Trump on this exact issue. Then, as I was waking up, I felt something touch both of my feet through the blanket. Mind you I was then wide awake. An angel touched my feet is my only explanation, as I was to remember the dream.

What is so interesting about the dream of the comet is that in the fall of 2019, while doing our radio show, a listener contacted me. She wanted me to listen to another radio show. In it a preacher from some 20 plus years ago had miraculously overcome what I understood to be a life-threatening situation. What she wanted me to listen to was that this preacher was then given a prophesy that a comet was heading towards the earth and that in particular it was coming our way because of all the darkness that had infiltrated the Roman Catholic Church.

The listener of course knew nothing of my dream or of my experience with the tornado of darkness that I saw within the Vatican. During our next radio show, my co-host Bart Chapman, and I talked not only about the caller's information but about my dream of the comet heading towards Earth, as well. In particular we discussed how we, as active members of the Body of Christ, can work to disperse any such massive object from space such that it will break apart into smaller pieces, similarly to what I saw in the dream. In fighting the battle between good and evil, God will allow whatever it takes to wake us up, and this could very well be a comet slamming into Earth. The more we are awakened and the more we are living a righteous life, as described in the previous chapters, the less likely such an event is necessary. For those of us who are inclined to not only purify our own bodies, but that of the corrupted portion of the Body of Christ as well, as previously described, now is the time to do so.

When editing the above in the spring of 2020 my friend John from the U.K. sent me a link to a podcast that featured a discussion on a planet known as Planet X. The speaker theorized that it has an orbit that takes it through our solar system every 3,600 years and that it is due back soon. Some say that it is what the King James version of the Bible calls Wormwood, or translated to Bitterness as written in the NLT. I found it interesting that without any knowledge of that theory I also named one of my dreams Planet X, as described later in this chapter. I do not know if the two are related.

The speaker then went on to say that there was absolutely no way that Earth would ever collide with their Planet X. But there would be with almost certainty a comet from that celestial system colliding with Earth. This got my attention, as my dream of a comet headed towards Earth and then at the last minute breaking apart, had a strong impact on me. This is not something to be tossed aside as nonsense.

The podcast was sent to me a few days after Easter in the spring of 2020. Early Sunday morning April 19, 2020, which is Orthodox Easter, I started to do some focused purification exercises. It went well but I wondered if there was something more. I thought of my dream and then of the podcast, and how the comet broke apart due to us raising our level of consciousness. I then thought I would try and tap into the energy field of the comet. Amazingly, I did and with very little effort! I was equally surprised that what I was experiencing was a deeper level of purification, a cleansing!

Just then I got a voice mail from John in the U.K. I did not want to interrupt my meditation so I clumsily sent a written text back telling him

I would listen later, as I was meditating. I then said for him to try and tap into the energy of the comet. He immediately sent back a text stating, "Listen to my message." So, I did. In it he was explaining that he had just tapped into the essence of the comet. He then went on to explain the colors of the energy that he saw in his own body. He also said it was a cleansing experience, the same word that I had used. He did so simultaneous to me, some 5,200 miles away.

The next morning, I thought about the comet, wondering if I could once again tap into its energy field. At some point in time I saw a small, bright red star in what I believed to have been the eastern night's sky. Its location was not of significance, but the fact that it was there, was. I took note of this and then continued with the meditative experience. Next I felt a release of a subtle anger that I was hanging onto for a couple of people that I knew. Accordingly, this was an emotional release.

Then I heard, "Evacuate the Vatican."

I was not in a dream state but was definitely connecting with the energy of the comet. We have all heard the old saying that God works in mysterious ways, and this is certainly one of them. But I tell you this, getting in touch with the cleansing power of the forthcoming comet is crucial, and it may be the single most important thing we can do in our lives. There is too much at stake to ignore this.

In talking with Barbara about the above I realized that what the energy of this comet is doing is, in fact, assisting in the raising of our consciousness. This occurs when we contemplate its significance and when we have discussions about it with our friends and neighbors. In doing so we connect with it and as a result elevate ourselves. This all happens at the spirit level. Accordingly, its necessity to slam into the planet to wake us up is significantly diminished. The comet breaking apart, either figuratively or literally, because of our elevated state of awareness, is exactly what I saw in my original dream. Fascinating!

Blue Kachina Red Kachina

A couple of days later I recalled that in the podcast the speaker had also briefly touched on the Hopi Prophecy called the Blue Kachina Red Kachina. He went on to give his explanation of their associated blue and red colors and how they might be connected to the coming of Planet X in its 3600–year cycle. The Hopi nation is in northwest Arizona, not far from where I live.

Using the Internet, I looked up information on the Blue Kachina Red Kachina. In all of the writings that I found each and every one stated that, "When the purifier comes, we will see him first as a small red star...," and that the "Purifier will bring the Day of Purification." Once again, I had confirmation of what I had experienced through my spirit. Recall that my friend John from the U.K. had said that what he felt was a cleansing and what I experienced was a purification. What I saw in my mind was a small red star all just as stated in the Hopi Prophesies. They continue to stress major earth changes. This too, is prophesized in the Holy Bible. There is much more information on the Hopi teachings and is available from several different websites. I encourage the reader to check them out.

> **Revelation 14:18 NLT**. *"Then another angel came, who had the power to destroy with fire, came from the alter. He shouted to the angle with the sharp sickle. Swing your sickle now to gather the clusters of grapes from the vines of the earth, for they are ripe for judgment."*

> **Revelation 16: NLT**. *"Then I heard a mighty voice from the temple say to the seven angels, "Go your ways and pour out on the earth the seven bowls containing God's wrath."*

Might this wrath be what the Hopi's prophesized as well? After all, God came to me without me owning or reading a Bible. He certainly could have done the same to the Hopi many years ago.

A few days after having the red star vision I was at a local restaurant picking up my takeout order. A woman in her mid-thirties was also waiting for her food. She explained that she had just recently arrived in the area. Her return trip home to Pennsylvania had been delayed because of the COVID-19 travel restrictions. She and the female hostess, whom I had known for several years, had hit it off and were talking of issues deep in nature. Something told me that I needed to say something to the woman just as she was getting ready to leave with her food.

"Hey, while you are here check out Blue Kachina Red Kachina," I said.

"What?" she asked.

"Blue Kachina Red Kachina," I replied.

She then looked at me and held up her arm. "Wow. I don't know what you are talking about, but whatever it is; it just gave me goose bumps. I'll definitely check it out."

My intuition was right. This woman was searching. I did not have the time to tell her all about my journey. But I did have time to tell her those few words and it worked. She will find God as she is capable of doing so. And this is what the calling is all about. My message to those who may not agree with my approach is:

Matthew 7:1 KJV. *"Judge not, that ye be not judged."*

Also written in the prophecies it states, speaking of forthcoming changes on Earth, "They will start as fires that burn within us, and we will burn up with desires and conflict..."

And that brings us to my next dream, The Dream of the Cleansing Fire, which I had about three years prior to reading about the Hopi's history.

Dream of the Cleansing Fire

In this dream I was standing on a grassy ridge. There were few if any trees and the grass was short and somewhat dry. There were small groups of people located at various locations. Looking around I could see dozens and dozens of specifically located fires on the surrounding hills and on the ridge which I was standing. I walked down the crest of the hill and came across a group of a half dozen people or more, and beyond them there was another group of about the same size. Each had a small amount of burns on them from the fires, not to any significant degree, except for perhaps one or two. But they would be okay.

Then, I came across a young woman, perhaps in her late twenties. She was lying on the ground in great pain. Her arms and other parts of her body were literally smoking as they were being burned from the inside out. Unfortunately, there was nothing I could do for her, as this burning from within was brought on by herself, by her actions in the way that she had lived. She was not a prostitute or addicted to drugs. She seemed like what many would think would be a normal young woman, but she had twisted her beliefs in God. I looked to the surrounding areas and realized that the dozens of fires that I could see off in the distance were for the same reason. Those who had lived unrighteous lives, those who were self- righteous, and did not believe in God or honor God, were also being cleansed by the fire.

After having had the above dream with the purifying fire I looked up the following verses:

> **Psalms 97:1-6 NLT**
> *"The LORD is king!*
> *Let the earth rejoice!*
> *Let the farthest coastlands be glad.*
> *Dark clouds surround him.*
> *Righteousness and justice are the foundation of his throne.*
> *Fire spreads ahead of him*
> *and burns up all his foes.*
> *His lightning flashes out across the world.*
> *The earth sees and trembles.*

The mountains melt like wax before the LORD,
before the Lord of all the earth.
The heavens proclaim his righteousness;
every nation sees his glory."

31:21-24 NLT. *"You must purify yourselves and your captives on the third and seventh days. Purify all your clothing, too, and everything made of leather, goat hair, or wood." Then Eleazar the priest said to the men who were in the battle, "The LORD has given Moses this legal requirement: Anything made of gold, silver, bronze, iron, tin, or lead— that is, all metals that do not burn—must be passed through fire in order to be made ceremonially pure. These metal objects must then be further purified with the water of purification. But everything that burns must be purified by the water alone. On the seventh day you must wash your clothes and be purified. Then you may return to the camp."*

And from Malachi:

Malachi 3:1-5NLT. The Coming Day of Judgment. *"Look! I am sending my messenger, and he will prepare the way before me. Then the Lord you are seeking will suddenly come to his*

Temple. The messenger of the covenant, whom you look for so eagerly, is surely coming," says the LORD of Heaven's Armies.

But who will be able to endure it when he comes? Who will be able to stand and face him when he appears? For he will be like a blazing fire that refines metal, or like a strong soap that bleaches clothes. He will sit like a refiner of silver, burning away the dross. He will purify the Levites, refining them like gold and silver, so that they may once again offer acceptable sacrifices to the LORD. Then once more the LORD will accept the offerings brought to him by the people of Judah and Jerusalem, as he did in the past.

At that time, I will put you on trial. I am eager to witness against all sorcerers and adulterers and liars. I will speak against those who cheat employees of their wages, who oppress widows and orphans, or who deprive the foreigners living among you of justice, for these people do not fear me," says the LORD of Heaven's Armies."

Malachi 4:1 NLT. *"The day of judgment is coming, burning like a furnace. On that day the arrogant and*

the wicked will, be burned up like straw.
They will be consumed-- roots, branches
and all. "

In Luke 3:16 Luke wrote about what John the
Baptist said:

Luke 3:16 NLT. John answered their
questions by saying, *"I baptize you*
with water; but someone is coming soon
who is greater than I am—so much
greater that I'm not even worthy to be
his slave and untie the straps of his
sandals. He will baptize you with the
Holy Spirit and with fire. "

Here again we see the word fire, and as Christ
comes to the people they must be purified, and
to become pure we are baptized in the fire. Of
all my dreams the Dream of the Cleansing Fire
was certainly one of the most foretelling. My
co-host Bart Chapman and I spoke about this
several times on our radio show. I said it then
and I will say it now, let us prepare.

Dream of Planet X

During the general time frame that I had the first
of the previously mentioned dreams I had what
was in ways the most profound one of them all.
In it I had been transported to and participated
in the dream, as if I was living it and living in it.
I was with a group of individuals that comprised
an away team. We had landed on a fairly

unknown planet at a predetermined landing site. To my surprise the entire area was completely decimated. There was absolutely no vegetation whatsoever, none, just red sand stone rocks, and some sand. There were absolutely no signs of life. The area was relatively flat with a wash like feature with a hard gravel bottom. A few miles off in the distance were some hills and then behind them some rocky mountainous areas. I was shocked as we were the second such group to land, the first having taken place several months before. The planet was to have been inhabited and advanced in its technology and thriving.

Of the group I was one of the captains, but there did not seem to be any one person in charge, so in a way everyone was a captain, with no one under them. One of the other captains, a female, pulled out a pistol like devise. It was made to transport through time any given area. Though because of its size it was limited as to how far back or how far in the future it could be effective, especially because I knew the entire planet was of a similar state.

I said something to the effect, "That won't work," knowing we had to go back even before the first landing team had arrived. Instinctively, I knew that that team had somehow caused the decimation that we were witnessing.

The down fall of our organization was that no given individual was in charge. Because of this I knew there would be no consensus as to what form of action to take, so I pulled out my bazooka looking shoulder held devise and shot us all back about three years in time. Immediately, I was well adapted to the local society, and I knew all of the others had automatically done the same. The difference being I was able to consciously observe the behavior of the other party members and that of the local civilization. From this I was able to access the local societal conditioning.

The planet then was thriving. The air was clean; there was no pollution, and basically no crime. As I watched members of our crew interact with the native people, I knew that the planet's citizens each had a specific role in what seemed like their perfect society. And it was in many ways truly perfect. I could not then tell what part of their society had not kept pace with their technological advancements. I did notice how two of our male crew members were walking down a sidewalk of a local business area. I also realized that since they too were captains that they did this on their own accord; there was no directive coming from a superior. This was the flaw in our own system, a society that strived to make everyone equal, whether they were capable or not.

There were one-story businesses buildings lining the street on both sides. The two members of our group mingled with the locals as if they had lived there their entire life. I also saw that they did not need to carry any identification on them, nor did anyone else. This was because the society was so evolved, and everyone was so honest, all you needed was to have some other citizen vouch for you. Thus, the two crew members could vouch for each other if ever they were approached by an official. Still, I knew there was something missing.

Suddenly, a young male member of our party, perhaps only 15 -years old, went screaming past me on a motorcycle, one made for the dirt trails. Close behind were about three police cars with their lights on and their sirens blasting. The young rider turned to his right down a residential side street, and then again to his left, and then once again to his right. The police cars were not as close as they had been before because of the skill that the young man had in riding the motorcycle. He took the sharp right turn at an incredible and seemingly impossible speed! Yet, the bike's wheels amazingly stuck to the pavement instead of sliding out. The young man then took another left-hand turn but this time there was a dead end, as there was a ravine about ten feet deep, and one hundred feet wide at the end of the block.

The police stopped their cars about half way down the block. Without slowing, the rider seemed to prepare to jump the ravine and land on the other side. The police chief came up to me and said not to be concerned. Then, he added that it was highly unusual for a citizen to act up like this. I realized that the police had probably anticipated that the boy was going to attempt to jump the ravine, but they had a surprise in store that they knew would safely capture the young man.

It was then that I came to know that most, if not all, of the advancement of the society on the planet had come from people learning to use their imaginations, while little was achieved because of believing in God. Yet, I was sure that they did believe in God, but their priorities were reversed. They strived to have a perfect society, one with no crime, absolutely no illness, and basically with little to no disagreements. They had evolved in many ways that you could say were in fact perfect. This is, in fact, a God given ability, to use our imagination to become more like Christ; more like God himself. But what they left behind was the humility to search for and get to know God at a much deeper level.

The surprise that the police appeared to have in store was a fine netting that, once the boy was in mid-air, would shoot out and capture him and the bike and gently lower him down. This devise did not seem to be a piece of equipment that the police carried with them, but it was created on the spot by their own imaginations. The Police Chief, and all of their society as far as that goes, was so confident that their methods worked that there was absolutely no doubt in their minds to the extent that unknowingly they based their entire existence on this belief. This being that their society was in fact perfect and that the methods by which they got to this level of perfection was infallible. Accordingly, the imagination of those in power, those in government, were the governing powers. No one could or would ever want to "out imagine" them, as there was absolutely no need in a seemingly perfect society.

The boy, with his surprising riding abilities, did not slow down as he approached the dead end. He easily lifted the front end of the bike into the air and off he went, flying across the ravine. Just as the police planned, when he got half-way across they fired the devise and the netting shot out and immediately surrounded the boy and his motorbike. With my abilities to observe others and tap into their minds I knew that what happened next put the police into a state of disbelief. The boy, with his own intuitiveness, seemed to have instantaneously imagined that the netting would unravel. And so it did and he continued to fly through the air and land safely on the other side.

It was then that I understood why the planet was decimated when our party first landed, some three years in the future. What the first landing party had done was similar to what ours had done; they fit right into the planet's society. They needed no identification, and at first, they made no noticeable impact. Then someone, like the young man riding the motorcycle in our group, disrupted their system. They out thought those in authoritative positions within their society. This put shock waves into the subconscious minds of those in government and eventually in the minds of all of their citizens. Bit by bit their projection of their own existence and roles began to crumble.

Upon realizing that their society which they had lived in for hundreds of years was in fact not perfect they had a mental breakdown. With this eventually came the images of a failed society and then a failed existence to the extent that what they saw was no existence at all. And that is what they then created, and that is what we found when we landed. Not only were our own people from the original landing party no longer in existence, but the life of the entire planet was gone, the people, the animals, and all of the vegetation. There was nothing.

Lessons from this dream were twofold. First, in the society of the landing party, of which in the dream I was a member, it had been mandated that no one person was in command, such that everyone was equal regardless of ability. As a result, each member of the landing party did their own thing. Since there was no protocol those without foresight made mistakes, and those with leadership skills were trained to not use it. As a result, the impact on the planet ultimately lead to its destruction, even though the planet was more advanced in many ways than the society where the landing party had come from. Second, was the fact that the people on the planet, what I called Planet X, put their own safety and comfort before that of knowing and seeking God. So evolved were they that they were as advanced as any society in that dimension could get. However, they did not continue their transformation of self into becoming even further of whom God made them to be, to becoming more God-like. This then led to their own destruction.

From this dream it is also clear that our imaginations are very powerful. Everything we as humans invent and create first comes from our imagination. As a structural engineer and an architect, every time I design a particular component of a building, I first see it in my mind. I know what it will look like, and how it will be sound in its design.

> **Genesis 11: 3-7 NLT.** *"They began saying to each other, "Let's make bricks and harden them with fire." (In this region bricks were used instead of stone,*

134

and tar was used for mortar.) Then they said, "Come, let's build a great city for ourselves with a tower that reaches into the sky. This will make us famous and keep us from being scattered all over the world.

But the LORD came down to look at the city and the tower the people were building. "Look!" he said. "The people are united, and they all speak the same language. After this, nothing they set out to do will be impossible for them! Come, let's go down and confuse the people with different languages. Then they won't be able to understand each other."

From the above the builders of the Tower of Babel first imagined the tower when they said, *"Come, let's build a great city for ourselves with a tower that reaches into the sky. This will make us famous and keep us from being scattered all over the world."*

Here we can see how God gave us our imaginations to create things in our lives, just as the young man used to outwit the governing powers on Planet X.

Also note that in Genesis 11 they all spoke the same language. When they could do this their abilities were limitless, but rather than seeking the Lord within themselves, their intent was to first provide for their own safety and comfort. They tried to achieve that by, as stated in Genesis 11, becoming famous! At no time did they stop to consider in humility who God is, and how they might become more like Him! Still, today we are scattered. We do not all speak the same when it comes to knowing God and understanding the Bible, let along speak the same physical language. In becoming more of who we were made to be; we will do much better at this. We can then use our imaginations to the extent that God has created for us to do, which, as stated in Genesis is limitless.

> ***Genesis 11:6 NLT***. *"Look!" he said. "The people are united, and they all speak the same language. After this, nothing they set out to do will be impossible for them!"*

The lessons to take away from this dream is to stop this ridiculous trend in our own society here on Earth to make everyone equal in all levels, especially in the work place and in athletics. We are all equal in God's eyes but we each have a mind, a free will, various abilities and a variety of circumstances in life and our life opportunities. This gives each of us as individuals the freedom to become whom we were made to be, each uniquely in who we are. Some of us are better athletes; some are more skilled at being a chef, while others are the best carpenters or teachers. From this we make up our own unique individuality in the Mystical Body of Christ, and this is who we must humbly strive to become. We must also place God first and our comfort second. In doing so, our comfort will come. Equally, we must unite in our quest to know God and use our imaginations to create the world around us.

Dream of Demons Being Purified

In the fall of 2019 Bart and I were giving our weekly "The Freeing of One Billion Souls" radio show broadcast. At a point in time after having the experience of being amongst hordes of the enemy, as described in the Battle in the Heavenly realms, I was intensely purifying my mind and body. I often do so by focusing on the thought of the word "purification." In doing this I indeed find my mind, and therefore my soul and body, being purified. That evening I had a dream where Bart and I had entered a building. It was a modular type of building, similar to a manufactured home or what is often referred to as a trailer. We had to climb a few steps to get to the entry door. Once inside, there was a small area, about the size of a standard living room. It had a bar off to the left. Bart and I walked through and then to the left, down a hallway. In the first room to the left there were a couple of attractive women. We then found ourselves in the bar area with the two women. I knew that they were women of ill repute and I was sure that Bart knew as well. Because of our purified state we could also see that they were demon-like in disguise. The one nearest me looked at me flirtatiously and was trying to entice me but my eyes easily penetrated her disguise. Her exterior began to fade away and expose what she was underneath. She became ugly and demonic looking. Then, that too disappeared and the human that she was before she had given into the devil began to appear. Because of my level of purification, with my eyes I was able to eradicate the devil's control over her, and bring out her true essence. Nearby, Bart was interacting with the woman who was trying to entice him. He was laughing, while knowing very well what was happening. He looked and me and said that I was to take care of the woman with him as well.

Later on, I had a very similar dream, where with my eyes I was able to penetrate to the core of the demon-controlled person and allow for them to see who they truly were. What is interesting is that something very similar happened in the Rick Joyner book, The Torch and the Sword. In it when the hordes of the enemy had reached the river of living water the forces of good had given water to the forces of evil. The evil ones stopped fighting, and those who had been human began to take on their human identity, and no longer looked like and were controlled by demons. This, in part, is what Christ's coming in his body is all about, to overcome all evil.

Dream of Earth Splitting

In this dream there was a meeting I was to attend at 10 PM but then I forgot about it. However, at the last minute I did remember and made it just in time. I then left, and soon afterward I was at my friend Jim's house, which used to be my home. Together Jim and I worked on a very involved mathematical problem until 2:00 AM. Next, we discussed the theory used behind the equations, and ultimately stayed up all night. At 9:00 AM Jim went with me back to the meeting that had started the previous evening at 10 PM. Just before getting there a photo appeared on my phone. It was a real time photo of the people in the meeting. Using their bodies, they had formed the shape of a polyhedron of some kind, perhaps what is known as a regular dodecahedron. I wondered how the photo had appeared on my phone, as it was as if I had been there and had taken the picture myself.

When we arrived, I walked into the room where the people were where the photo had been taken, which was on the second level. The room was about 1,000 square-feet in size and had no furniture. The participants had just moved out of the polyhedron shape that they had made using their bodies. It was apparent that they had maintained that shape all night long for the entire time that I was with Jim. What was also extraordinary was that I too had been in the room with the rest of the participants while at the same time I was with Jim at his house working on the mathematical problems. It became obvious that there were two of me. I called all of the people together, including Jim, as they were gathering their things and getting ready to leave. I wanted all of them as witnesses to the fact that to the people in the meeting, I had been with them all night long, and equally clear to Jim and to me was that I had been with him during the same time frame. When I woke, the sensation of having been in two places at the same time was still with me. I thought about the equations that Jim and I were working on and of the polyhedron that the people's bodies had made. Clearly, the two were connected. I believe that they had to do with the science behind the phenomena of bilocation, which is further discussed in Chapter 8.

After waking from this first dream I quickly fell into a second. There were two very high cliffs on each side that were made of solid rock. They went straight up and had a suspension foot bridge spanning between the two sides. On it, about 80% of the way across the bridge from the left to the right was Daphne, Jim's wife.

I then spoke out loud, "I will not leave Daphne behind." And then woke up.

My interpretation of these two dreams is that we are preparing for the coming of the Lord, and that in doing so we will evolve to levels now not understood. Also, when it comes to the concept of bilocation, there is a science behind it, one that we have yet to discover. In addition, there will indeed be two worlds, the new Earth and the old Earth. The old being that which we are now living. And that it is up to us to span between the two worlds and take as many people as we can with us to the new. Please note that there have been numerous well documented cases involving various Catholic saints, as is presented in Chapter 8, that have had bilocation experiences.

Dream of Becoming a Christ

Early in the morning of May 20, 2020 I woke while having a profound experience. At one point in this dreamlike state there were two of me, both equal, both a Christ. I use the term "a Christ" because I do not want people to become confused by what I mean. In this experience I was completely equal to Christ in each and every aspect. This is what I believe we are to become.

> **Ephesians 4:11-13 NLT.** *"Now these are the gifts Christ gave to the church: the apostles, the prophets, the evangelists, and the pastors and*

teachers. Their responsibility is to equip God's people to do his work and build up the church, the body of Christ. This will continue until we all come to such unity in our faith and knowledge of God's Son that we will be mature in the Lord, measuring up to the full and complete standard of Christ."

And from **Romans 8:29-30 NLT.** *"For God knew his people in advance, and he chose them to become like his son, so that his son would be the firstborn among many brothers and sisters. And having chosen them, he called them to come to him. And having called them, he gave them right standing with himself. And having given them right standing, he gave them his glory."*

The above being said, to me this is our ultimate goal, to embody our spirit such that we are a Christ, just as Jesus is.

And from **John 17: 20-24**. *"I am praying not only for these disciples but also for all who will ever believe in me through their message. I pray that they will all be one, just as you and I are one—as you are in me, Father, and I am in you. And may they be in us so that the world will believe you sent me.*

142

"I have given them the glory you gave me, so they may be one as we are one. I am in them and you are in me. May they experience such perfect unity that the world will know that you sent me and that you love them as much as you love me. Father, I want these whom you have given me to be with me where I am. Then they can see all the glory you gave me because you loved me even before the world began!"

In the above it always strikes me that Jesus was certainly wanting the same that he had with the Father for not only the disciples but for those who will believe through their message. The only way possible for this to happen is if we too are a Christ.

Chapter Seven

The Next Step to Closing the Devil's Door

Closing the Devil's Door

> **Corinthians 8:1-3.** Paul wrote, "...*But while knowledge makes us feel important, it is love that strengthens the church. Anyone who claims to know all the answers doesn't really know very much. But the person who loves God is the one whom God recognizes.*"

> **2 Peter 1:2.** Peter wrote, "*May God give you more and more grace and peace as you grow in your knowledge of God and Jesus our Lord.*"

It is the word knowledge that I want to discuss with you, as the more we have of how the universe works, the better we can close the devil's door and get closer to God. However, as stated, we are not to think that somehow such knowledge makes us greater than others, as it does not. But it can help us to understand the ways of the universe and therefore the ways of the devil. Remember, it is Satan that does not want you to become who you truly are, and that is someone who meets the full and complete standards of Christ. See Ephesians 4:13.

Knowing the distinction between Spirit and Soul is part of this knowledge.

> Peter goes on to say, "*Growing in Faith By his divine power, God has given us everything we need for living a Godly life. We have received all of this by coming to know him, the one who called us to himself by means of his marvelous glory and excellence. And because of his glory and excellence, he has given us great and precious promises. These are the promises that enable you to share his divine nature and escape the worlds corruption caused by human desires.*"

I believe we all must grow in our knowledge. In Lesson 7, I introduced the distinction between the human spirit, soul, and body.

> Recall that in **Thessalonians 5:23** Paul states, "*...and may your whole spirit and soul and body be kept blameless.*"

To better understand how to close the devil's door we must further our knowledge. Knowing the distinction between soul and spirit and understanding the makeup of each is an important part. Our spirit is not only a creation of God, but I believe it is made in his image, and contains much of his wisdom. Our spirit is guided by and filled with the Holy Spirit, the Spirit of God. The human soul is made up of a portion of the mind, and our will, and emotions. It is also given to us by the Father. However, our minds and emotions can be influenced by our free will, and thus subject to be influenced by the devil. The mind consists of our thoughts, will, intentions, and our personalities. The mind, and in particular our personality, interacts with and is directly connected to our emotions. There is a lack of spiritual knowledge in this area, not only within the Christian community, but in most all spiritual communities. However, some mystics, even non-Christian ones, are aware that the soul is made of the emotions and the mind, with some calling our spirit the over-soul, or other terms, as previously mentioned. It is important to realize that in the Bible the spirit is called the spirit, so that is what I am calling it. The wording is quite clear.

What has been studied to a certain extent is the scientific connection between our minds and our emotions. The reader can feel free to research that information as much as they like. The information I am giving is more on the spiritual level, that which cannot be seen with the naked eye, nor studied scientifically. When we have some sort of trauma in our lives it creates a void in our emotions. A part of the soul is then left behind. However, the impact can be healed, especially when invoking the Holy Spirit, and with simply placing love onto it. However, until that occurs the mind remembers the trauma. There is an electrical charge associated with that memory. When situations similar to that which caused the trauma come up, that memory in our minds is triggered, and that electrical charge sends out a warning signal that our emotions react to. It is important to heal that trauma, as depending on the significance it can have serious symptoms. These are evident in our veterans who suffer from PTSD. In children, the symptoms are similar to ADHD, and often they are misdiagnosed and are treated for ADHD, instead of healing a traumatic memory.

Until the trauma is healed our reaction is to do all we can to avoid the emotional feeling that comes from the memory. An event causing such a condition does not need to be as profound and obvious as that which our veterans have experienced in war. For example, if early on in our childhood we had a very reactive parent, one that jumped at almost anything, we as young children learned to avoid that situation as we did not want the upset to come in our direction. Thus, we learned to avoid confrontation and then seek approval. To get the love we wanted we began to believe we needed to please people so that they would not be angry with us. There are many variations of this type of reaction. Some adults want to argue and confront those that have upset them while others avoid the confrontation all together. Either way, these tendencies become part of our personality.

Each time we react because of these often long-forgotten memories we are not being the person that God created us to be. And now to a very important point. It is when we react with these emotions that the devil's door is opened to our soul. Satan does not want us to be consciously connected with our spirit and become the powerful individual that we are meant to be!

> **Romans 8:29-30 NLT.** *"For God knew his people in advance, and he chose them to become like his son, so that his son would be the firstborn among many brothers and sisters. And having chosen them, he called them to come to him. And having called them, he gave them right standing with himself. And having given them right standing, he gave them his glory."*

The Distinction Between Soul and Spirit

Just as we were completing the Catholic Church and school engineering project that we designed in Flagstaff, Arizona, I was invited to attend a meeting in a nearby town where we watched videos of various ministers, and then discussed what we thought of them. The first series was by Andrew Wommack, whom I mentioned earlier.

He has an entire teaching on the distinction between Spirit, Soul, and Body. The revelation that he received on the subject directly corresponded to my own experiences and understanding that I had had some 16 years earlier. He actually has produced a 20-minute animated DVD that quickly and effectively covers this most important information, or perhaps better said, knowledge.

It was during this period in time that I discovered the following verse in the Old Testament.

> **Isaiah 9:6-7 NLT.** *"For a child is born to us, a son is given us. The government will rest on his shoulders. And he will be called: Wonderful, Counselor, Mighty God, Everlasting Father, Prince of Peace. His government and his peace will never end. He will rule with fairness and justice from the throne of his ancestor David for all eternity. The passionate commitment of the Lord of Heaven's Armies will make this happen!"*

The child Isaiah is referring to is certainly Jesus. Therefore, the armies he is referring to are the armies to come, not those in the Old Testament.

> In **Psalms 103:19-22** David wrote, *"The Lord has made the heavens his throne;*

from there he rules over everything. Praise the Lord you angels, you mighty ones who carry out his plans, listening for each of his commands."

I ask, are you one of his angels? The Lord is revealing to us the knowledge needed for this to come to be. Using this to throw out the devil from your life will have a supernatural effect and do the same in the lives of others. This is when the Lord will govern here on earth, when the devil has been removed.

Psalms continues with, *"Yes, praise the Lord you armies of angels who serve him and do his will!"*

You see, the Lord wants us to be strong and knowledgeable disciples. He wants us to pave the way for his coming. I suspect that without us doing our part it would be much more difficult on all of us when he does come, and how he comes, speaking of the Body of Christ.

In **Ephesians 1:21** Paul says, *"Now he is far above any ruler or authority or power or leader or anything else-not only in this world but in the world to come."*

I now better understand what the message from my spirit meant when it said, "You are going to overthrow government," as described in later chapters when my spirit spoke to me for the third time.

I now understand it to mean, "By becoming who you are, who you are in God, you will be doing your role in fulfilling the Lord's Prayer when it says,

> *"Thy kingdom come thy will be done on Earth as it is in Heaven."*

When the Kingdom of God has fully come to Earth, Christ will govern all of Earth. That is how we overthrow government to make way for the Kingdom of God.

> Paul continues with **Ephesians 1:22**, *"God has put all things under the authority of Christ and has made him head over all things for the benefit of the church. And the church is his body; it is made full and complete by Christ, who fills all things everywhere with himself."*

It now is becoming clearer, as we become aware of Christ, of his message and who he is, we become like Christ himself and fill ourselves with him, with God and with our own spirit, all in one. And if Christ governs over all things and we are filled with him then we will govern over all things on Earth!

A person might ask, "I understand that there are portals that allow access to our minds and emotions, or soul, and that it would certainly be in our best interest to close these off. I also understand the distinction you have made between spirit and soul, but why is it important to make that distinction?"

> Recall that in **Ephesians 6:10-12** Paul said, *"A final word: Be strong in the Lord and in his mighty power. Put on all of God's armor so that you will be able to stand firm against all strategies of the devil. For we are not fighting against flesh-and blood enemies, but against evil rulers and authorities of the unseen world, against mighty powers in this dark world, and against evil spirits in the heavenly places."*

In the above the armor Paul is referring to is faith in Jesus Christ and the knowledge that is used to remove the devil's influence from our lives.

> In **John 6:63** John states, *"The spirit alone gives eternal life,"* and in Romans 7:6 it states,*"...Now we can serve God, not the old way of obeying the letter of the law, but in the new way of living in the Spirit."*

To live in spirit, we must make way for it to come into us. It is then the Holy Spirit, through our spirit, that will influence our souls (our minds and emotions). To achieve this, we must not allow the devil to have access. We can now take the next step in doing what the Lord wants of us, and that is to reconnect the spirit with the soul on a full-time and conscious basis. It is with that direction and knowledge given us that our minds and emotions can accomplish what the Lord wants us to do. It is through the Living Water that will then flow through us that will reconnect the spirit and soul!

In **Romans 8:4-17** Paul wrote, *"He did this so that the just requirement of the law would be fully satisfied for us, who no longer follow our sinful nature but instead follow the Spirit.*

Those who are dominated by the sinful nature think about sinful things, but those who are controlled by the Holy Spirit think about things that please the Spirit. So, letting your sinful nature control your mind leads to death. But letting the Spirit control your mind leads to life and peace. For the sinful nature is always hostile to God. It never did obey God's laws, and it never will. That's why those who are still under the control of their sinful nature can never please God.

But you are not controlled by your sinful nature. You are controlled by the Spirit if you have the Spirit of God living in you. (And remember that those who do not have the Spirit of Christ living in them do not belong to him at all.) And Christ lives within you, so even though your body will die because of sin, the Spirit gives you life because you have been made right with God. The Spirit of God, who raised Jesus from the dead, lives in you. And just as God raised Christ Jesus from the dead, he will give life to your mortal bodies by this same Spirit living within you.

Therefore, dear brothers and sisters, you have no obligation to do what your sinful nature urges you to do. For if you live by its dictates, you will die. But if through the power of the Spirit you put to death the deeds of your sinful nature, you will live. For all who are led by the Spirit of God are children of God.

So, you have not received a spirit that makes you fearful slaves. Instead, you received God's Spirit when he adopted you as his own children. Now we call him, "Abba, Father." For his Spirit joins with our spirit to affirm that we are God's children. And since we are his children, we are his heirs. In fact, together with Christ we are heirs of God's glory. But if we are to share his glory, we must also share his suffering."

This is when we begin to feel the Love of Jesus and God the Father at a much deeper level than ever before.

Let us remember that in **1 Corinthians 8:1** Paul states, when speaking about food that has been offered to idols, *"Yes, we know that "we all have knowledge" about this issue. But while knowledge makes us feel important, it is love that strengthens the church ... but the person who loves God is the one whom God recognizes."*

Accordingly, with all the information I am giving in this book, nothing supersedes the love that we can have for God, and all knowledge is secondary!

Satan wants to keep us from getting God's glory and power. The devil wants to keep us disconnected from our spirit. He does this by entering our soul, that is our minds and emotions, through portals hidden behind the reactive areas in our personality. These weaknesses are not always, but are often caused by the emotional upset described. Because these personality traits are so commonplace, we have become to see them as part of our true selves, when they are not. Due to the fact that these portals are hidden so well the devil can strongly participate in our lives without us even knowing it!

Please listen carefully. You do not need to be an alcoholic, a drug user, or a criminal to have Satan influence your life. You can go to church every Sunday and to Bible study during the week. You can be a good neighbor and a loving parent. You can be an involved citizen in worldly ways and at times still be influenced by Satan without your knowledge. This keeps you from becoming all that God made you to be. It can come up in our inability to have complete and total forgiveness for those who have hurt us, or in the way we look at others who we disagree with. Are you placing agape love onto them to the best of your ability? If not, something is keeping you (us) from growing in spirit.

In "The Dream of the Fall," that was included in a previous chapter; it described the darkness that covered the planet when the Fall of mankind took place. God knew what had happened as giving free will to his creation would ultimately lead to a fall when the humans were influenced by temptation. The Fall resulted in a separation of mankind from them in God. This was a result of Satan being allowed to influence our minds and emotions, or our soul. Our spirit is still a direct image of God, as it was made to be so. Therefore, it has not been tainted by the influence of Satan. But its ability to come through us has been greatly diminished and in some cases completely cut off. This is the separation that took place, a disconnection of the soul from our spirit. When we are in touch with our spirit we are in touch with the Holy Spirit and therefore in touch with God, our creator.

> In **Ephesians 1:19** Paul said, *"I also pray that you will understand the incredible greatness of God's power for us who believe him. This is the same mighty power that raised Christ from the dead and seated him at the place of honor at God's right hand in the heavenly realms."*

We have not achieved the power that God is speaking of because we have separated ourselves from God. The devil wants us to remain that way and does all he can to try and keep us down. He does not want us to become who we are, that being powerful individuals made in the image of God. For the most part we have not learned about Satan's tactics and therefore we have not learned how to close the door on those tactics. Because our soul is not governed full-time by our spirit, and because Satan is so clever in his ways, all of us are under the influence of Satan to one extent or another. Do not be alarmed. God knew this would happen when he gave us free will. It is part of

God's plan for us to simply become aware of this and mature ourselves as Christians.

There is a lack of knowledge and understanding of how the blind spots or weaknesses in our personalities allow the devil to enter our lives through these portals. He and his demons then manipulate our minds and emotions, which, again, is our souls.

> In **John 6:63** he states, "*The spirit alone gives eternal life*" Note that he did not say the soul gives you eternal life. He continues with "*...the very words I have spoken to you are spirit and life.*"

This takes us right back to Lesson 3, the Power of the Word. Our words when spoken from spirit is life! When spoken from the devil's influence through our minds is death. By manipulating our minds and emotions the devil keeps us from connecting with our spirit and allowing it, in union with the Holy Spirit, to govern.

> In **James 3:6** it states, "*And the tongue is a flame of fire. It is a whole world of wickedness, corrupting your entire body. It can set your whole life on fire, for it is set on fire by hell itself.*"

In this verse the words from our tongues has been influenced by the devil. It is important to understand that when we give access to the devil, to our lives, we do and say things that hurt others and ourselves. Note that this verse ends with, *"for it is set on fire by hell itself."* This means exactly what is says. The devil far too often has influence over what we say, as we unknowingly have given demons direct access to our souls. This is not to say that we cannot be in touch with and hear from our spirit from time to time, typically at crucial points in our lives. But by allowing such we go back and forth from being in touch with our spirit to letting the devil in, especially when we are angry.

> This is evident from **James 3:9** speaking of the tongue, *"Sometimes it praises our lord and Father, and sometimes it curses those who have been made in the image of God. And so, blessing and cursing come pouring out of the same mouth."*

We can overcome this tendency when we know how the devil works.

> Continuing in **James 3**: he states, *"...Such things are unearthly, unspiritual, and demonic."*

Note that James used the word "demonic." This is a strong word and not used lightly. When we let the devil in, we let demons into our world.

James also wrote the word "unspiritual." Here he is stating that it is not spiritual to act with the influence of the devil.

> In **Ephesians 6:18** Paul states, *"Pray in the Spirit at all times and on every occasion. Stay alert and be persistent in your prayers for all believers everywhere."*

Why would Paul say this?

> In **Ephesians 6:17** he states, *"Put on salvation as your helmet, and take the sword of the Spirit, which is the word of God." It is clear that to fight the devil we use the word of God. And when we do this with persistence, we do it not only for ourselves but for all believers everywhere."*

Note the word *"everywhere."* God's ways are many and supernatural. We do not know nor have experienced the immensity of it all. Here, we have the Word stating to pray in the spirit and to do it for all believers.

What this means is that when we pray in spirit all believers benefit. We all get kicked up a place or two in our journey to fully understanding God's word. Please note he did not say, "pray in soul." He said, "pray in spirit."

Equally from **John 4:24.** *"For God is Spirit, so those who worship him must worship in spirit and in truth."*

Again, note when talking to the Samaritan woman in this passage Jesus did not say, *"worship (the Father) in soul,"* he said, *"in spirit."*

The soul is a part of our minds and our emotions. The spirit it that which is created in God's image. I experienced this first hand in my healing, as described in earlier chapters. This is supported in the Bible.

> In **Romans 12:2** Paul says,"...*let God transform you into a new person by changing the way you think.*

This is very important to understand. The way we think governs our spiritual progression. Yet, too often the way we think is under the influence of the devil through the use of the portals.

> In **James 3:17** it says, *"But the wisdom from above is first of all pure. It is also peace loving, gentle at all times and willing to yield to others..."*

If we are not living like this, we are not as mature Christians as we need to be and have not yet learned how to Close the Devil's Door.

162

In **Romans 7:6** it states,"...*Now we can serve God, not the old way of obeying the letter of the law, but in the new way of living in the Spirit.* "

In the days that we are now living in, it is essential that we learn to do this, to live in spirit. But we cannot do so without realizing that not only does God exist, but Satan is real, and we unknowingly give him access to our souls. This knowledge has been before us in the Bible for the last two-thousand years but most all Christian churches do not teach the distinction between soul and spirit. We can better Close the Devil's Door by understanding this information and using it and the insights that God has given us to do so.

In **Ephesians 6:10-12** Paul said, *"A final word: Be strong in the Lord and in his mighty power. Put on all of God's armor so that you will be able to stand firm against all strategies of the devil. For we are not fighting against flesh-and blood enemies, but against evil rulers and authorities of the unseen world, against mighty powers in this dark world, and against evil spirits in the heavenly places."*

In the above Paul was well aware of the devil's tactics. Using the information revealed in this book we can put on our armor and arm ourselves with the knowledge and the tools to crush the devil. Having done so, we can ensure that we will be governed with the knowledge of our spirit, and not by the devil influencing our minds and emotions, or our souls.

In **Romans 8:6** Paul states, *"So letting your sinful nature control your mind leads to death. But letting the Spirit control your mind leads to life and peace."*

Here Paul is speaking of the Holy Spirit, but remember God speaks to us through our spirit, and our spirit is joined by God's Spirit.

Romans 8:16. *"For his spirit joins with our spirit to affirm that we are God's children."*

Note that in **Acts 2:41 (ESV English Standard Version)** it states, speaking of Peter, *"Those who received his word were baptized, and there were added that day about three thousand souls."*

These souls were saved and no longer governed by ignorance and subject to the ways of the devil.

In **Matthew 16:26** it states, *"And what do you benefit if you gain the whole world but lose your own soul?"*

Here, the ways of the world taint the soul and again you lose it to the ways of the devil. Matthew is speaking of losing your soul which is your mind and emotions, not your spirit.

Now that we know the distinction between spirit and soul, we can move on to learning more on how to close the unseen portals to our souls.

Casting Out the Devil

In the fall of 2019 a loved one, whose name I will give as Jackson, had been listening to various sermons where he realized that he must change the way he thinks. Andrew Wommack, for example, has a great series on this subject. Soon after having this realization, Jackson, while having a conversation with me, stated that in fact he was going to change the way he thinks. Soon after making this statement, on a Monday as I recall, he told me that he began to feel a bit off in his stomach. The next morning the feeling was worse, and his appetite was not good. By evening the symptoms were even worse.

On Wednesday morning he said that he had slept very little, was in serious pain in his solar plexus, and could not eat or drink water. He had put an early call into his doctor's office with no one following up. By 10:00 AM we decided it was time to go to the ER as the symptoms were getting worse. The long story short, after 7 hours in the ER with a CAT scan, an ultra-sound, and an IV for fluids, we had no answers. They sent Jackson home with enough opiates to last for three days.

The next day I took him to see his doctor. He reviewed the CAT scan and the ultra-sound and came to the same conclusion, there was no medical explanation for the severe pain and inability to eat or drink. Jackson, seeing no other way, asked to be admitted to the nearby hospital. There, the doctors also reviewed the same tests, then performed some of their own, along with asking routine questions. They too had no answers as to what was causing the condition, but agreed to keep him in the hospital for observation.

That night the pain was just as severe and Jackson needed at least four doses of pain medication to get through the night. Around 6 AM the following morning, a Friday, Jackson woke. I had spent the night in the hospital with him. He was once again in great pain, as the medication was wearing off and he was still unable to eat or drink, though they had given him an IV for fluids. The choices were few. If they sent him home once again with just a few pain killers what was he to do? Keep coming back to the ER? The pain pills they were giving him were opiates. Soon he would be addicted and how was he to nourish himself?

I stood up and looked at Jackson and said, "You said you wanted to change the way you think. Well now is the time to do it!"

We had both listened to Andrew Wommack's lessons on speaking directly to the health issue, and how when we pray not to beg God, but to speak to the problem. Jackson also stood up and I looked him in the eye and then down to his solar plexus area.

I said, "Pain I am speaking to you, I am speaking directly to you. I cast you out!"

I had done several radio shows on how Jesus gave us the authority to heal the sick and cast out any demons.

> **In Luke 9:1** Luke wrote, *"One day Jesus called his twelve disciples and gave them power and authority to cast out all demons and to heal all diseases."*

It is clear that in the Bible we all have that authority, as we are to, "meet the full and complete standards of Christ." Ephesians 4.

Jackson, feeling as if he had no other choice but to take that authority that God has given us, then said, "Lies exposed, liars exposed, I cast you out in the name of Jesus!"

He was sticking to his guns, as a few days before he had stated that he was going to change the way he thinks. The pain he was undergoing was not going to alter that declaration! He had to change the way he thought about the world and about God because, like all of us, he had been exposed to the ways of the world for his entire life! For example, though he believed in God, he of course had also been influenced by the messages of the movies he had seen (some good and some bad), by the media, by participation in social media (as younger people are these days) and by every other influence of the world.

> In **2 Corinthians 4** Paul wrote, "*Satan, who is the god of this world, has blinded the minds of those who don't believe.*"

Jackson did believe in God but as his faith grew stronger Satan did not want to let go of his influence.

Recall that demons utilize portals to access our mind, which is a part of our soul, and therefore our thoughts. These portals can be of a whole variety. As discussed, often they are through our insecurities. And too often they come from us being overly concerned about what others think of us or how we present ourselves via social media or any other means.

> In **1 Peter 5: 8-9** Peter wrote, *"Stay alert! Watch out for your great enemy, the devil. He prowls around like a roaring lion, looking for someone to devour. Stand firm against him, and be strong in your faith. Remember that your family of believers all over the world is going through the same kind of suffering you are."*

The devil had certainly been prowling around as he knew that Jackson would have an impact on the world. This would be fully participating in God's plan. We do so by speaking out about God and how important it is to know that God resides within each person. And also, how important it is to answer the calling to become who God has created us to be!

Our commands of speaking directly to the pain and the lies and the liar had a substantial impact. Only a few minutes had passed when Jackson looked at me and said, "The pain is gone!"

Jackson, having found such great reward and relief, went back to bed to rest. I then sat back down on the lounge chair that the hospital staff had set up for me and continued to pray. After a while I too drifted off. When I woke up a couple of hours had gone by and Jackson was sitting up in bed ordering his breakfast! This was the first time in over three days that he had an appetite.

After eating a healthy breakfast Jackson said that the pain was coming back a little so we prayed once again, casting out the liar, the lies, and the discomfort. Our prayers became more assertive. Once again, we spoke directly to the pain and to the liar. After another thirty minutes or so Jackson said he felt much better than he had in days.

"I am going for a walk," he said. He walked through the hospital corridors for over two hours, something he could not even have imagined just the day before.

The doctors were of course happy that he was doing so much better, but had no idea as to why. We did mention prayer to one of the nurses and she said that that was a good thing. She of course had not had the direct experience that Jackson and I just had. Therefore, she did not realize the importance of this kind of prayer. That night the pain came back somewhat and Jackson, not wanting it to get severe like it had before, asked for one dose of the pain pills. Recall that the night before he had a total of four. This was a big improvement.

The next morning, a Saturday, the pain was making its way back and we did the prayers again. Once again, we had good success.

Jackson ate his second full breakfast in the last two days. By noon they had released him from the hospital and I drove him home.

What Jackson and I had gone through over the prior five days was intense, from the ER room, to his doctor's office with still having no results, and then our stay at the hospital.

He was doing fine and I needed a break. So, I said, "I am going on a motorcycle ride with Barb. I will check in on you later."

What is interesting is that when I get on my motorcycle with Barbara, I feel free and, I will say, invulnerable. And trust me, I say this humbly, as riding a motorcycle is typically not the safest mode of transportation. It was fall out in November of 2019. The air was crisp yet it was warm enough to have a good ride. After about a forty-minute ride, I decided to take a side road. It was a two-lane paved road, typically with little traffic.

We were on this side road for less than a minute and traveling at about 40 mph. All of a sudden my handle bars wobbled three times. Simultaneously, I saw the head and eyes of a deer looking up at me from under my right foot peg. My foot really hurt and I let out a holler as I let off the accelerator. The best I could tell a full-sized deer had slammed into the right side of my motorcycle.

As I slowed down, I lifted my right foot up off the peg.

Barbara heard me yell out, "My foot, my foot!" "What's wrong?" she asked.

It had all happened so quickly she did not know we had hit a deer, as it seemed to come from out of nowhere. Neither one of us saw it leap from the side of the road, and there was little to no vegetation present.

I pulled off of the road onto a wide spot. I was afraid to look at my foot, as it had taken a significant amount of the impact. I looked down and it was fine and incredibly the pain was completely gone. There had been a black Cadillac SUV following behind us with a man and his wife inside. The driver stopped next to us and rolled down the passenger window.

"Man, are you okay?" he exclaimed.

"Yeah, I'm fine. Was that a deer I hit?"

"Yes, it was," he said.

"Is it alive?" I asked.

"No man, you laid it out. It's dead." he replied. Seeing that we were okay, he then drove off.

I turned the bike around to go see the deer. It was half in the drive lane and half off. It had blood coming from its mouth and gave a last kick before it died. Barb and I looked at it for a few seconds and then I drove on. The intensity of what had just happened was unprecedented. When I got home, I told Jackson about what had taken place with the deer.

"What time did it happen?" he asked.

I told him.

Then he said surprisingly, "Wow, just about that same time I was holding a glass and for no reason at all it dropped from my hand and fell to the floor, shattering into many pieces."

It was right then and there that he and I agreed that God was indeed calling us and that it was important that we pay direct attention to that calling, just as we did when Jackson was in the hospital. And even though he was doing so much better we were not to go back to the way we were living. As each and every moment had to be in thought of and all inclusive of God in our day to day lives.

Jackson was staying with me at that time. We found that each night the pain would start to come back and Jackson's appetite was being challenged again, but not anything like it was before. At first his reaction was to take a pain pill. Realizing that this was no way to live, I would get up and we would intensely pray together. Often, this lasted for up to an hour and was anywhere from 3 or 4 AM. This went on for a couple of weeks, with the nighttime being the most intense. The prayers worked, more and more so each night, and after about two weeks the pain was completely gone. The appetite, though not yet normal, was stabilizing. We realized that the pain that was in the solar plexus area was where there had previously been anxiety. This is one way in which the devil can access our being. If you think about it, being who God meant us to be certainly does not include feeling anxious. What it does include is being humble and confident in who we are, regardless of the situation we find ourselves in.

What we found over those few weeks is that the devil will do all he can to keep someone from growing into being more like Christ, and becoming whom God made them to be. This will include demonic attacks up to the degree that Jackson had encountered. The tactics used are numerous and include every part of your being that they can gain access to. These include the impact that social media has had on you, incorrect important historical facts (all part of the lie), and the twisting and misrepresentation of God's word by too many of our churches. Methods used also include aspects of our culture and any misguided societal beliefs on sex or any other subjects. Especially if these beliefs and influences direct a person away from knowing God, which ultimately, they would have found within themselves. Our prayers included closing down all portals that the devil could access.

During our prayers we each spoke with the authority directly to the source and said the following:

"Access denied. Portals closed. I cast you out Satan."

Then I would continue with something like, "I cast you out of Jackson's mind, out of his thoughts and out of his beliefs. Portals closed! Access denied!"

There is a good book by John Bevere called, Access Denied.   In it he writes about such portals. But the methods that Bevere espouses are somewhat different than what we did.

A short time later Jackson came across a conference on spiritual warfare on YouTube. A Father Ripperger of the Roman Catholic Church gave the presentation. As it turns out Father Ripperger is one of the most knowledgeable and capable priests that I have come across on this subject. He explained in detail what the devil is up to and the tactics used. Much of his talk had to do with possession, which the situation with Jackson was clearly not. We knew this all along, but the reasons behind the attacks are similar.

I have said over the years that God will never allow you to be in a spiritual situation such that Jackson went through that you cannot overcome. Father Ripperger confirmed this. With all his years of experience in this arena he stated how no demon can attack a human without God allowing it. It is not that God wants it, but he does allow it. This is because when you fight a battle as Jackson did, with my assistance at first, you gain in virtue. This is important when answering the call from God. To gain in virtue is to acknowledge things that are true, noble, just, pure, lovely (as Christ is), and things of good reports of people doing good things for God. When we then speak of such things we speak with confidence and valor.

Father Ripperger went on to tell of Satan's kingdom, how it works, of his four top generals and how when in battle when a demon gives up; they will provide you their name. They are now in your control. In the following section you will see how the demon Whitan gave her name to me when I captured her. Seeing this presentation by Father Ripperger was confirmation of what Jackson and I went through and verified why he had to go through it. His calling is big, and the battle was difficult, but the virtue that he has gained has given him the tools that he now needs to do God's work for him here on Earth. Satan did not want Jackson to prevail, as he knew that he would do much good for the world in doing God's work. Looking back, having had that challenge has played a major role in making him who he is today.

About twelve weeks after it all began; I was having a conversation with Jackson about various religious beliefs and the various denominations. We did not necessarily agree on each subject but we did concur when it came to the importance of taking out Satan wherever he or his helpers are found.

I then remembered an event of some years earlier when upon awakening I had sensed that there was some sort of Satanic activity in the general vicinity. At the time I was in Marin County, California. My spiritual warrior self immediately went into action. Using a radar like detection I located and then disabled that energy. I then had a vision of a powerful wolf high upon a cliff, looking out over the area below, watching for any reactivation of any such practices. I related this experience to Jackson. We then both felt that by having had that discussion we were in fact doing the same. We were taking out Satan wherever he was hiding and removing his influence away from whomever he was attempting to control. This is doing God's work. It is our job to close the devil's door on our own lives. Those around us will benefit, and so will our country, and therefore the world.

I know this is how I will overthrow government as discussed in the following chapter. I do the work on myself and I let God do the work on others. It is when we have Godly people in government that are armed with faith and true knowledge that we can improve our country. Remember, transform yourself and you will have an impact on the world around you.

Demonic Bugs

Recently, I was listening to one of my favorite preachers. He was telling the story of when he had a problem with his ear, as apparently it had a significant case of skin cancer. In my opinion this man is about as close to God as we can humanly get. Eventually, by speaking directly to his ear, it was healed without going to the doctor. But prior to this a reverend friend of his said that he saw hundreds of tiny ant-like demons around his ear, trying to make their way in to his being. These demonic bugs could not affect the preacher because of his strong faith. Nor did he succumb to the ways of the world as far as relying on modern medicine, but instead went to the authority that God has given us that we find within ourselves. This is a good example of how these tiny demons try to get in, and often do, and begin to damage our bodies and influence our minds.

In the Dream of the Fall what came out first from being locked up for a very long time, perhaps thousands of years, were the flying black bugs. These, along with the other creatures, were evil. They all work for Satan. In Lesson 7 I described how I found bugs trying to eat away at my soul. I knew they were very damaging to my energy field but had not directly associated them with Satan. Also, after exposing them by purifying my mind I was able to remove every single one of them. Now, having read about such things in portions of the Bible and knowing more about Satan's ways it makes perfect sense that these bugs were in fact demonic.

In another situation I had been working on helping a young man become who God made him to be. Like most all young men these days he had been influenced by his share of Satan's means through the media, society, and pornography. It is pornography that is Satan's most effective weapon and it is the demonic bugs that do most of this work for him. In this particular case while I was praying for this young man, I sensed an energetic disruption in his being, or as some say in his energy body, or better said in his soul. At the time I was several hundreds of miles away. I felt as if energetically this disruption needed to be grounded out so I did just that. We can do this by thinking and by stating it to be so, remember the power of our word in Lesson 3.

Soon I drifted off to sleep and when I started to wake in spirit world, I saw a horrible site. There was possibly a couple dozen of different types of bugs hidden away in and disrupting this young man's energy body. There were green ones, black bugs and some beetle looking ones, and they were all so very ugly. Each of the beetle looking bugs were carrying balls of a black colored mass which I believe was their food, I am sure harvested from this young man's energy field. These balls were approximately 2" in diameter and then when the bugs got to the hole in the dirt that lead down to their nests, they would release the balls so that they would roll down the hole and into their nests. All of the various bugs had holes in the ground several inches from each other that lead to their nests. All were climbing in and out of the holes, like ants do. With my foot I disrupted some of the dirt, energetically of course. Instantly, dozens of very tiny bugs came flying up out. They were similar to those described in the Dream of the Fall, but much smaller.

I then spoke directly to all these demons and commanded that they and that Satan be gone! The next morning, I wrote the young man and told him what had happened. Together we cast out Satan and all his helpers. By discovering the bugs and by casting out the devil, and repeating that all portals were closed, and that all access was denied, we crushed their nests and killed them all.

It is this kind of knowledge that we need to know so that we can better fend off Satan. He uses all of these methods to try and keep us from answering our calling and to then become who God made us to be.

A Demon Gives Herself Up

About three years prior to the experience with Jackson I had had a discussion with a very perceptive person about becoming a more mature Christian. She had the ability to see demons and send them on their way. Sometimes she would notice the presence of a demon when we were speaking. I was more than curious about following up on what she had to say. At that time throughout my spiritual experiences I had sent several ghosts to God who were trapped here on Earth. As mentioned earlier in the text I had discovered that those who had committed suicide were particularly prone to being stuck. I had encountered at least one large demon as well, all of whom I simply sent them to God.

This time it was different, as I had not sensed the presence of any ghosts, spirits or otherwise. Even so, I respected this woman's insight so that evening I decided to cast a net out in the nearby area. Sure enough, I felt like I had caught something. I typically do this work at night and soon I was drifting off to sleep. I then had a very clear dream. I was in my house, not my physical house, but that which represents my spirit house. Sitting at the dining room table was a man that I knew well as a teenager, whose name was Richard. I had not seen him in over forty years. I was surprised, as even though I was happy to see him, I was a bit flustered as to why he had let himself into my home without calling, writing or even knocking. He was just there!

It was then in my dream that I felt that uneasiness that comes from being in conflict, my shortcoming at that time as I have previously mentioned. Even though I was in a dream-like state I was awake enough to recognize that feeling. I knew I had to deal with the awkward situation by being clear with Rich. I had to tell him that I was uncomfortable with the fact that he had let himself in. Rich and I were sitting across from each other. As I was speaking to him, I noticed a ruffling at the end of the table to my left. I walked over to investigate. I then noticed that there was something hidden under a camouflage that had been placed over the end chair. I looked closely and to my surprise there was a demon underneath the cloth. By not being distracted with my tendency to avoid conflict, and therefore confronting my friend directly, I had disrupted the hidden nature of this devil's helper.

The demon was a female. Upon being discovered she looked up at me and gave me her name.

"Whitan," I heard her say in a scratchy like voice.

She then got up and walked towards the entry then turned left and down a hallway. Near the end of the hall there was a door on the right, but she continued to the dead end. There, she revealed to me a hidden portal. It was through this passageway that she, and I am sure other demons, had access to my life! I knew what it was and fully intended to thrust my hand and arm into the portal and not only close it but extend the Light of God into it. I felt a resistance so I pushed harder and as I woke my arm thrust forward. In doing so I had sealed off this portal.

The next day or so I was in my kitchen while I had EWTN on, the Catholic television station. On the program they were interviewing a Catholic priest. As part of his job he cast out demons from people. He was quite nonchalant, as it simply was part of his everyday job. He then said when the demons gave him their name, they had given themselves over to Jesus! This is exactly what had happened with me. I had indeed cast a net out and captured a demon. When I confronted my insecurity of avoiding conflict with the man that had let himself into my home, Whitan became exposed. It was then that I had control over her and she then showed me the portal. These openings into our being are placed or hidden behind our insecurities. It is very clever to do so because it is when our feelings of discomfort click in that we are not that which God made us to be. Our God given abilities are compromised and the demons come and go unnoticed.

I cannot over stress the significance of this. Every person on Earth has a personality glitch of one kind or another. Accordingly, all of us are subject to these demons entering our world and influencing our minds and emotions, or our souls. It is our souls that Satan wants. If we do not give it freely through the use of drugs, alcohol, crime, hate or anger, we certainly give him influence through our insecurities. Remember, with the Fall came the separation of the spirit and the soul, and it is through these portals that Satan manipulates us and keeps us from having and knowing that God is fully within us. But it is when we kick Satan out, we then allow for our spirit to be in us. It is then we can begin to have all the promises that God gave us, including having the power that rose Jesus from the dead.

From Ephesians **1:18-20 NLT**. Spiritual Wisdom: *"I ask that the eyes of your heart may be enlightened, so that you* *may know the hope of His calling, the riches of His glorious inheritance in the saints, and the surpassing greatness of His power to us who believe. He displayed this power in the working of His mighty strength, which He exerted in Christ when He raised Him from the dead and seated Him at His right hand in the heavenly realms."*

Satan does not want you to have this knowledge, as in doing so it exposes him and his tactics. As you read this you are exposing him and he is fleeing.

In **Luke 10:18-20** after the seventy-two disciples returned Jesus said, *"Yes", he told them, "I saw Satan fall from heaven like lightening! Look, I have given you authority over all the power of the enemy, and you can walk among snakes and scorpions and crush them. Nothing will injure you. But don't rejoice because evil spirits obey you: rejoice because your names are registered in Heaven."*

You too have authority over all the power of the enemy. Now that you know where to look you can use that authority and seal up these portals. However, you must deal with and confront your own insecurities and personality issues to keep these doors permanently closed. It may take a bit of practice but you will get there.

Covid-19 and the Protests in America

In the early part of the year 2020, the corona virus started to spread worldwide. European countries were among the first to close restaurants and museums, especially in Italy. In the United States several governors recommended the cancellation of any gatherings of 250 or more. As the virus continued to spread this number soon became only 10. Eventually churches were mandated to cancel their services and restaurants were told they could only prepare food for takeout. During the early months the entire San Francisco Bay Area shut down all but essential services like police, fire, hospitals, banks and grocery stores, impacting approximately 7 million people.

What is interesting is the public's response. I witnessed grocery stores in Texas having to close their doors early and hire armed guards because of the overwhelming crowds. Within 24 hours of the panic buying, the stores were back to normal, less their paper goods, especially toilet paper, bottled water, and several canned foods. This scenario was replicated throughout much of the U.S. I do understand not wanting to be inconvenienced by not having any toilet paper. However, what message are we giving here? What is happening in the bigger picture? Not surprisingly, too few thought more about God and instead thought more about themselves. Fortunately, several local churches did organize and prepare to help those in need. As one parishioner stated, "It is an opportunity for them to put into action what they preach, that being people who care about their communities whether those they serve believe in God or not." And when I say God I mean the God within. After all, there are those who struggle with the word God, for reasons discussed in earlier chapters, yet they still did not panic. These individuals are secure within themselves, and likely know God in their own terms, but speak of it in a different way than others may do.

But is this all there is to it? Is this virus simply another health issue that science can resolve, or is it more? I say at the minimum, it has been an opportunity for each individual to reflect upon themselves to determine what is important in their lives, and what is not. My hope is that from this reflection millions of people from around the world will realize that good resides within each and every one of us. And that this is where we need to look, humbly, within ourselves. In doing so we begin to find God, perhaps for the first time, or perhaps at a deeper level than ever before. It is during times like these that we can make a difference. Not only by helping others and by not panicking, but by transforming ourselves and therefore the world around us. These types of worldwide emergencies are an opportunity for transformation. Which do you choose?

As the shutdowns continued I had numerous conversations about the virus with friends and family. We discussed whether or not we should wear masks and gloves when we went out, and if businesses should be forced to shut down. After quite some time what I concluded was that the role of government is to provide as much accurate information as possible, and then give recommendations on how to deal with the situation. It then needs to be up to each individual as far as how to act in such circumstances. Each business owner needs to be able to decide for themselves if they are to remain open, or not, and how to maintain a healthy environment if they do stay open. Each person needs to decide whether or not they choose to wear a mask and gloves, understanding that we need to respect the requests of others if we choose to do business or interact with them. Unfortunately, in my opinion governments around the world overstepped their bounds when it came to the aforementioned. On the other hand, not all people are ready to look deeper into themselves and therefore could act irresponsibly. Either way, the situation has pushed people in one direction or another, an important decision by all that needs to be made. My family and I say a prayer almost daily. It is a command and what we say is, "No virus shall live upon our skin or in our body!" Amen.

Psalm 91, *"Those who live in the shelter of the Most High will find rest in the shadow of the Almighty....For he will rescue you from every trap and protect you from deadly disease."*

Recall that our words are powerful. By stating that no disease will live in our bodies we mean just that. If we do get ill, then we simply have not been residing in the shelter of the Most High.

Then in the spring of 2020 protests broke out all across the U.S. and in other parts of the world over the death of George Floyd, an unarmed black man that died while being taken into custody by the Minneapolis police. Once again the citizens of the United States of America found themselves on opposite sides as far as how to react to such an event. The tensions were increased because of so many being cooped up in their homes and not able to work due to the Covid-19 shutdown. Some believed that the riots and looting that followed were justified, while others saw it as anarchy.

After having several debates with my friends and others from both sides I have come to my own conclusion. I say that these two events, the Covid-19 outbreak and the riots of 2020, are not just coincidental. At some level they are related. I predict that the subsequent civil unrest is just the beginning of what is only going to get worse, especially after the presidential election of 2020. This being said, God has a plan and we are all part of it. And having respectful debate is an important part of that process.

> From **Revelations 3:15-19** John wrote, *"I know all the things you do, that you are neither hot nor cold. I wish that you were one or the other! But since you are like lukewarm water, neither hot nor cold, I will spit you out of my mouth! You say, 'I am rich. I have everything I want. I don't need a thing!' And you don't realize that you are wretched and miserable and poor and blind and naked. So I advise you to buy gold from me—gold that has been purified by fire. Then you will be rich. Also buy white garments from me so you will not be shamed by your nakedness, and ointment for your eyes so you will be able to see. I correct and discipline everyone I love. So be diligent and turn from your indifference."*

Anger and The Civil Unrest of 2020

When Donald Trump was elected as the president of the United States of America in 2016 the response on the political left was overwhelmingly negative. There was rioting in Washington D.C. Four letter words were used on national television followed by obscene hand gestures. Never before had I witnessed such anger when it came to a presidential election. Over the following four years the disrespect grew. White House staff member Sarah Sanders was denied service at a local restaurant, conservative television pundit Tomi Lahren was spat upon, a teenage kid had his cap knocked off while other supporters of the President had water thrown in their face. Most surprisingly was that Democratic political leaders such as Maxine Walters, Hillary Clinton and others continued to call for more disrespect and civil unrest against Republicans.

I asked myself and others why the excessive anger? I believe that the answer lies within each of us, and in particular in those who are acting out. What unresolved issues are there within us that brings forth such anger? What emotional blockages are we harboring? We are at a crossroads in this country. As stated in the above quote from Revelations 3: 15-19, we must decide which side we are on. Are we on a path that leads to a greater self that will ultimately resolve these issues or are we on a self-serving path that leads to supporting or participating in disrespect and even violence? What is most interesting is that the radical left is providing the opportunity for those who oppose this behavior to stand up for what they believe in and to not only pick a side but to speak out in support of that belief. This is important for all of us to do.

We all have a narrative of what life in this country should be like. When Donald Trump speaks, it rattles those on the left. This is because what he says counters their narrative. Too often they get angry, and in 2020 that anger came out in the riots where looting and other destructive behavior took place. Christ wants us to decide where we stand. By his actions Donald Trump is providing the opportunity for us to make that decision. No longer can we sit on the fence. We must pick one side or the other. Do we choose to find the part of God that lies within ourselves and become who we were made to be, or do we choose to act out in anger because our narrative is not only being challenged but possibly wrong? We are faced with challenging times. The power to transform this nation lies within each and every one of us. We must decide where we stand, inform our selves accurately on the subject at hand and voice our opinion respectfully. We must also be prepared to admit that we were wrong if the evidence is clear that we were, in fact, not on the right track. Recall that when what we have to say is in alignment with what it is our spirit wants us to say we will have an impact in the transformational process, as this is how it works. Our words are important.

.

What I have observed is that the emotions of those who resort to violence is what gets in the way of reasonable thinking, both on the far right and left. Recall, our emotions are a part of our soul and that is subject to be influenced by the devil to do evil. And do not get me wrong, Donald Trump is by far not a perfect individual, but he is playing a key role in the transformational process of this planet. God created us to become exactly like Christ. It is our minds and emotions that are keeping us from evolving. It is opportunities like that which we now have here in the United States of America that we must take advantage of. Remember, monitor your emotions and speak out.

Chapter Eight

Knowledge With Faith and Humility Gives Ability

From **James 3:13-17 NLT** we read *"True Wisdom Comes from God."*

"If you are wise and understand God's ways, prove it by living an honorable life, doing good works with the humility that comes from wisdom. But if you are bitterly jealous and there is selfish ambition in your heart, don't cover up the truth with boasting and lying. For jealousy and selfishness are not God's kind of wisdom. Such things are earthly, unspiritual, and demonic. For wherever there is jealousy and selfish ambition, there you will find disorder and evil of every kind.

But the wisdom from above is first of all pure. It is also peace loving, gentle at all times, and willing to yield to others. It is full of mercy and the fruit of good deeds. It shows no favoritism and is always sincere. And those who are peacemakers will plant seeds of peace and reap a harvest of righteousness."

From **Ephesians 1: 1-17 NLT** under Paul's *Prayer for Spiritual Wisdom* we read, *"That the God of our Lord Jesus Christ, the Father of glory, may give unto you the spirit of wisdom and the revelation of knowledge of him."*

This too means exactly what it says, may God give us revelation and knowledge of him. This is a very powerful statement. By using the word *revelation* Paul is telling us that the depth of the word of God is revealed to us. Without these revelations, we cannot grow as Christians, and neither can our church leaders and religious institutions teach these revelations, if they themselves do not receive them. And they will not receive them if they are not continuously reaching to learn more about God.

In **Romans 1:9** in the King James Version we read, *"For God is my witness, whom I serve with my spirit in the gospel of his Son, that without ceasing I make mention of you in all my prayers."*

In the NLT it substitutes the word "heart" for the word "spirit." Either this was an oversight or the translators did not understand the significance of the word spirit. I am sure that when Paul said, *"whom I serve in my spirit,"* he meant just that, as he knew the significance of his spirit. This is evidenced in Romans 8, subtitled *Life in the Spirit.*

> In **Romans 8:15-17** it states, *"For you have not received a spirit that makes you fearful slaves. Instead, you received God's Spirit when he adopted you as his own children. Now we call him, "Abba, Father." For his Spirit joins with our spirit to affirm that we are God's children."*

In the above, Paul clearly states that we have a spirit. Remember that in **Ephesians 6:18** Paul wrote, *"Pray in the Spirit at all times and on every occasion,* and this is what he meant. Not only do we have a spirit but God's Spirit joins with our spirit. It is very important to know that when we put love directly onto our pride, or our ego, we extinguish our pride and are then able to better be in touch with our spirit. This is when we find ourselves in the House of the Father and know that our renewed spirit truly does indeed reside there. Yet, it is still our individual spirit. It is important to know we have a soul and we have our own individual spirit. Again, one that resides in the House of the Father. The soul is subject to influence by the devil, but the spirit is not and it is joined with that of the Father. Being in touch with our spirit is how God's messages are revealed to us. Thus, we gain knowledge and become more mature Christians. With knowledge and faith, we gain more ability to do God's work.

In **Romans 10:1-3 KJV** Paul wrote, *"Brethren, my heart's desire and prayer to God for Israel is, that they might be saved. For I bear them record that they have a zeal of God, but not according to knowledge. For they being ignorant of God's righteousness, and going about to establish their own righteousness, have not submitted themselves unto the righteousness of God."*

I ask, has organized religion fallen into the same scenario? My answer is too often yes, but I encourage the reader to come to their own conclusion.

In **2 Corinthians 8:7** Paul wrote, *"Since you excel in so many ways-in your faith, your gifted speakers, your knowledge, your enthusiasm, and your love from us..."*

Here too Paul knew that knowledge of getting to know God better is so very essential.

We Must Change the Way We Think

Romans 8:5-6 Paul wrote, *"Those who are dominated by the sinful nature think* *about sinful things, but those who are controlled by the Holy Spirit think about things that please the Spirit. So, letting your sinful nature control your mind leads to death. But letting the Spirit control your mind leads to life and peace."*

Romans 8:10-11. *"And Christ lives within you, so even though your body will die because of sin, the Spirit gives you life because you have been made right with God. The Spirit of God, who raised Jesus from the dead, lives in you..."*

Romans 8:12-17. *"Therefore, dear brothers and sisters, you have no obligation to do what your sinful nature urges you to do. For if you live by its dictates you will die. But if through the power of the Spirit you put to death the deeds of your sinful nature, you will live. For all who are led by the Spirit of God are children of God.*

So, you have not received a spirit that makes you fearful slaves. Instead you received God's Spirit when he adopted you as his own children. Now we call him, "Abba", Father. For his Spirit joins with our spirit to affirm that we are God's children. And since we are his children, we are his heirs. In fact, together with Christ we are in God's glory..."

In the above Paul made it clear that we are the heirs to God's glory, and that it was God's glory that raised Jesus from the dead. But to receive that glory in its fullness we must rid ourselves of our sinful nature. To do this we must close the door to the devil such that he no longer influences us.

> **Romans 8:23** Paul wrote, *"And we believers also groan, even though we have the Holy Spirit within us as a foretaste to future glory, for we long for our bodies to be released from sin and suffering. We, too, wait with eager hope for the day when God will give us our full rights as his adopted children..."*
> **2 Peter 1:2** Peter wrote *"May God give you more and more grace and peace as you grow in your knowledge of God and Jesus our Lord."*

It is a piece of this knowledge that I want to share with you. Understanding the distinction between Spirit and Soul, which we covered in the previous chapters, is an important part.

> Peter goes on to say, *"Growing in Faith By his divine power, God has given us everything we need for living a Godly*

life. We have received all of this by coming to know him, the one who called us to himself by means of his marvelous glory and excellence. And because of his glory and excellence, he has given us great and precious promises. These are the promises that enable you to share his divine nature and escape the worlds corruption caused by human desires. "

The glory that Paul and Peter are speaking of is immense. It raised Jesus from the dead. It is there waiting for us to be able to do the same, but how do we get there? Might it be also through a better understanding of something like quantum physics and how God created that for our knowledge and use to be like Him?

There is so much in this phrase that we could talk for a week. However, let's focus on knowledge and faith. Faith without knowledge will not get you to the highest place you can be while here on earth. Faith with knowledge can start you on your way. What promises has God given? Among many things it includes the power to raise the dead!

Today, here on Earth, with faith alone we do not have the power that Paul is talking about. But with faith and knowledge we can begin the next phase of our journey to *know God* and more fully receive his glory.

Christ did not reveal himself to me until later in my journey. Though I certainly had prayed to Jesus, I did not have the connection I was thinking must exist if it was the real deal. It was not until sometime later that I felt the fullness of his Love. For thirty years I believed strongly in God. I prayed every day, often several times per day, to try and find this essence that we call God at a deeper level. I did not think a lot about Christ, as the presentation of Jesus during the few times I went to church did not do much for me.

Over the years I came to know many things about the universe and had numerous interdimensional experiences. It is not the intent of this book to go into detail about these experiences but having had them better prepared me for taking the next step in fulfilling my God given purpose. Again, we all have a purpose in life. It is when we begin to fulfill that purpose that we achieve great joy and fulfillment in our lives.

In 2017 I was lying in my bed when the most amazing feeling of love engulfed my entire body. As I started to wake, I thought, *I have never felt so much love.* I then became fully awake and knew that Christ himself had been by my bedside! This was my first experience with Jesus. Several months had passed. Then a loved one was diagnosed with cancer. This news was devastating, as he was quite young, still in his twenties. I prayed so very much for this young man to the point where it seemed to consume me, as his cancer too was supposedly incurable. At the time this young man did not have the faith that I did when I went through my illness, thus he had chosen to go the medical route. Early one morning I had a dream where I saw a tub, perhaps 3 feet wide in each direction, and the same in height. I saw where this steel like tub was immaculately clean almost throughout, but not down at the bottom in the corners, where the dirt is hardest to get out. This tub represented the young man's body and his cancer. Our prayers were doing much good but they were not strong enough in themselves to complete the job. I then saw the corners miraculously being cleaned and knew it was Christ that had done so, thus cleansing all cancer from the man's body. I also realized that Jesus did this in response to the man's mother and my prayers. The next night this dream was confirmed by another. I saw the young man in the tub but this time it was made of heavy-duty clear glass. He was sitting in it naked with his knees to his chest. All of the tub was immaculately clean. I knew he was healed. To this date no signs of the cancer have come back.

With the above, as I began to understand and accept Jesus for whom I understood him to be, things started to change and the Lord revealed even more mysteries to me.

Mark 4:22 NLT. *"For everything that is hidden will eventually be brought into the open, and every secret will be brought to light. Anyone with ears to hear should listen and understand."*

To better understand the beginnings of me getting an insight into the knowledge and experience that I am speaking of I need to go back a few years to the time of my own healing from cancer. After being supernaturally healed my spirit spoke to me for the third time. In 2003 my spirit told me telling me that I was going to overthrow government. I was perhaps the most excited I had ever been in my life. Well, maybe not as much as when I got my first deer while hunting with my dad when I was 14 years old. Or not as excited as when my dad bought me my first motorcycle a few months later. But probably nothing could make me more excited than that. Anyway, as I have written several times, for many years of my adult life I have felt strongly that I had a purpose. Hearing that purpose spoken to me from spirit and therefore in union with what we call God was, needless to say, impactful, and at times puzzling.

At that time, I had attended a five-day conference where many speakers came to present their experiences with healing and spirit, which I have previously mentioned. This was not a Christian based conference, yet many of the speakers were wise in their methods. On the last day of the conference some young people gave an impromptu talk on the art of dance. In particular it was dancing to electronic music. That night they had an event so those who wanted could experience what it was they were talking about. It was not about how good you looked or how cool you looked on the dance floor, it was about expressing yourself, your soul, through the movement of your body. I was attending the conference by myself and had no desire to dance with a partner. So, I took to the dance floor by myself. The first couple I saw dancing was one of the speakers, a songwriter who had written for the band The Grateful Dead, and his young European girlfriend. My first instinct was to look real cool, or at least think I would be, as this is what ego wants us to do. However, having recently gone through the experience with my healing I knew this was not the answer. I thought of what the young man who had given the presentation had said, to express yourself. What happened next caught me by surprise. Years earlier I had taken the martial art form of tai chi. What came out in my dance was every martial art style I had learned, but modified to a dance. The event lasted several hours, until past midnight. I danced to every song without taking time to rest. Drenched in sweat I had completely expressed myself from the inside out, the warrior within me. I was the last person to leave when the music eventually stopped.

That night I slept very well. The next morning while walking to the closing day of the conference I saw the two young men who had held the dance approaching me. For a moment I caught myself thinking, *Oh no! What are they going to think of me dancing like that?*

Then as they passed by one of them said, "Hey, there's the dancer."

And then the other said, "Yeah man, that was right from the soul!"

Of course, they get it, I thought, *They invented this stuff.*

That afternoon as I was driving out of the parking lot and ready to head home my spirit spoke to me for the third time, just as clear as the first time.

In complete union with God our Heavenly Father I heard, *"You are going to overthrow government."*

Never before had I heard or felt such an impact on my spirit, soul, body mind and emotions. For the first time I heard what a major component of what my purpose was. I was in an altered state of being during my six-hour drive home. Over the following days my question was, how was I going to do this? How was I going to accomplish such a task? As I believe in nonviolence and I do not think that protests do much good. It was not until autumn of the year 2016 that I began to understand.

However, first I need to go back to the year 2011 and expand upon you how important it is to express ourselves freely. That is when I was hired by a local Catholic parish to design a new church, administrative building, and school. We wanted to incorporate exposed, decorative concrete floors into the design. There was a convention in Las Vegas that had displays of just about anything you need in the concrete construction industry. Accordingly, the priest, two parishioners and I drove to Vegas, about a five-hour drive. During our drive I told myself to simply be myself and speak my truth, as I was sure we would have some differences in our spiritual beliefs and experiences.

At that time, it had not yet been revealed to me how the devil snuck his way into our lives through the portals hidden behind the weaknesses in our personalities. The trip to Vegas and back went well and we all got to know each other much better. When I arrived home, my spirit spoke to me again, saying, *"You are overthrowing* government!" It is not often that I hear such profound messages. When I do, I have learned to listen carefully. Looking back on the day's journey I realized that my spirit spoke these words to me purely because I was as open as I could be while on the road trip. I held nothing back, while of course being as respectful and courteous as I could be. I simply presented myself for who I am, and nothing more or nothing less.

The subtitle of this section is to change the way we think, and in doing so to minimize the impact that the ways of the world has on us and maximize the way that the Spirit can act through us. By doing so, when doing so humbly, we can impact the world around us.

My spirit twice more spoke to me while giving me the same message. The third time I heard this message was when I was out to dinner at the airport restaurant in Sedona. A couple from out of town had sat down next to us at the bar. Once again, I held nothing back, to be my complete self and to talk as if I were talking to God himself. I did just that, though I do not remember the specific conversation. Again, while sitting there, spirit came through telling me, *"You are overthrowing government."*

The fourth time was just as I was preparing to hike down the Grand Canyon with a high school friend. While standing on the rim of the canyon I was on the phone with another friend, who goes by the name Windtalker. I openly and clearly expressed to Windtalker how important it was to fully express ourselves. Then, right there on the south rim of the Grand Canyon, it came through again, *"You are overthrowing government."*

When we change the way we think, we let go of all false perceptions of how we believe we need to act, to dance or to speak in a way that might somehow give that person a good image of ourselves. In doing so our true selves comes through. We then bring our spirit and therefore God into the atmosphere of where we are speaking. This is very important to understand.

Another example of lessons that we might need to learn in order to be who God made us to be can be seen in the experiences I had while designing the Roman Catholic school and church, as previously mentioned, in Flagstaff, Arizona. The funds to build out this Catholic Church and school project were not immediately available. Therefore, designing and building the project was phased over a period of five years. It was during this period that God was preparing me to know Jesus at a much deeper level. The Lord was well aware of an area of my personality that needed to be strengthened. As in the past I would go out of my way to avoid conflict and too often seek approval from others.

In the first three years of the project there were two individuals that I had a significant conflict with. One was over an engineering design issue and the other about project management of the construction process. The details are not important to explain, but the feeling in my gut was so strong with one instance that I had a tough time talking; I mean I was stuttering over my words. Nonetheless I stuck to my guns, and said what it was I needed to say, in the most respectful way I could, of course. The person I am now speaking of, that I had a conflict with, ended up being a good friend. She was a true Godsend to challenge me in the way she did. Without her I would not have had the opportunity to grow the way that I did.

The second instance involved another engineer challenging my work. As it turned out I was right, and he was wrong, there was no two ways about it. This was more complicated than it might seem up front, and for other reasons I choose not to elaborate any further. It would have been easy to acquiesce and give in to the wishes of the other person but I chose not to. This individual and I are not friends and I have not heard from him since. Too bad, as I am sure God has a role in all of this for him as well. Well, maybe what has come of it is his role, I do not know. Sticking to my guns regardless of the threats was important for me to do. I knew it was not only in the best interest of the project to not simply give in, but it was in my own best interest to not back down. In the end things turned out fine and the project was successfully completed. However, these two circumstances were major tests for me. Fortunately, I passed.

I realize that other people have other areas in their personalities that may need improvement, and conflict with others may not be it. Nonetheless, for me at that time this was a very big deal. I did pass the test and did so without being aware of how the devil pulls at our weaknesses. Accordingly, I got much better at dealing with this type of situation, but not to the point of feeling all of God's glory as a person can once they learn to close the devil's door from all of their life. In short, to do God's work to our fullest ability we need to get through our issues and become the strong individual that God originally created us to be. To achieve this, we need knowledge.

Christian Mysticism

Most of the information that I have given in this book is based on direct experiences that I have had in the spiritual realms. I am typically not much for titles but to classify this kind of interaction it is often referred to as Christian mysticism. During our radio show in 2019 my co-host and I broadcast an entire show on this subject. We did so because there is a lot of confusion around this term, especially from many Protestant pastors. Once again, and sadly, many Christian pastors were not taught anything about this subject when they went to seminary. They then think that anyone who has these kinds of experiences or talks about such things are not well versed in Biblical matters. Intentionally, they cast doubt onto the authenticity of those that might have Christian mystical experiences. This is sad, as these pastors are too often being ridden like horses and used by the enemy, as pointed out so clearly in Rick Joyner's books. I am going to write further about this subject to try and clear things up, not only for the reader but hopefully for those pastors who do not understand as well.

Earlier in this book I described how my spirit, in union with God's Spirit, spoke to me. First, I heard that it was okay to love myself, as described in Lesson 3. Second, it was God through my spirit telling me that the reason for my illness was now over, as described in lesson 9. Then again when God through my spirit told me I was overthrowing government, some four times. These are all examples of having a Christian mystical experience. I say Christian as they are in union with God our Heavenly Father and with Christ.

The three steps that I took when I heard that the number of souls that will pass through the Body of Christ was one billion were 1) to place non-narcissistic love onto myself, 2) purify my thoughts and 3) disperse my ego, or pride, by placing the energy of love onto it. A short time after I had the revelation that it was one billion souls that would be released from captivity, I was watching EWTN, the Catholic television network.

Once again I was watching "Father Spitzer's Universe" on EWTN. That night he was talking about Christian mysticism. What he described was that throughout the history of the church there were mystics within the church, such as Saint Teresa of Avila, Saint John of the Cross, and others. He then went on to describe that all of the Christian mystics had one thing in common, and that was how they went about going into their mystical state. All had written that it involved three things. The first being to place some element of non-narcissistic love onto themselves, the second was having a significant amount of purity, and the third involved minimizing their ego. Needless to say, I was glad to hear the commonality between these Christian mystics and the procedures that I discovered.

Also note that I often say that God spoke to me through my spirit. The first time this happened was when I was ill. It was when I heard that, "it was okay to love myself," as described in Lesson 3. I say "through my spirit" as that is how God communicates with us. In particular I felt this when I heard the words, "Brent, it's okay to love yourself." It was so clear, and it was my voice talking to me, it was a greater me talking to me! At the time I did not know what to call this "greater me," and, as mentioned, I had heard it being called the "over soul," so I used that for a few years. But when I started reading the Bible, I realized this is our spirit, as described in previous sections of this book.

As I was watching Father Spitzer's Universe on EWTN about Christian mysticism he described that this is how God talks to us, that being through our spirit. Once again, the experiences that I had were confirmed with Christian mystics of the past.

So how do we deal with those pastors who do not understand the term Christian mysticism? We treat them like we would all people. We emanate love and have patience, and do not ridicule them. Remember they are a member of our body, so they must be treated with love.

Further Purification

Continued purification on a daily basis is so very important. Sinful thoughts and a memory of past experiences can easily pop up in your mind. You must immediately respond with a cleansing process, as a demonic entity can attach itself in one way or another. An easy way to reverse any such experiences is to simply start saying your favorite prayer or the Lord's Prayer. For Catholic's the Hail Mary can also be used. The Hail Mary is actually quite effective and to my Protestant friends please do not prejudge, as the Hail Mary is clearly not praying to Mary, it is asking for prayers, just as you ask a friend for prayers. Remember, sin is simply an act by which we do something that diminishes our connection with our spirit, and therefore with God.

Saying the aforementioned prayers will give quick results. The devil and his demonic helpers cannot stand to hear the Lord's Prayer spoken to them, or other prayers, or the praising of Christ. By reciting these you may find that you have netted yourself a demon and delivered it to God for Judgment. At a minimum you will rid yourself of any, in essence, self-inflicted wounds that the demonic bugs or otherwise can cause due to those sinful thoughts. If you catch yourself having a damaging thought, with the most harmful typically being sexual in nature, be persistent. Go after the devil and his helpers, and do not stop until you rid yourself of their influence. You will know when this happens as a feeling of purity will fill your mind. Purification is so very important, especially during these times of our calling. We simply cannot complete God's work through our part of the Body of Christ without it.

Recently, one such scenario happened to me. I was indeed being persistent in pursuing the devil or one of his demonic helpers. I did corner him, but was not sure if I had completely cleansed myself. Some time had passed and my focus wandered a bit. I had a brief thought about my retirement and of the financial needs that I will have at that time. This was as brief as the sentence I used to write about it. I then remembered I had been pursuing a stuck energy and immediately I went to thinking, *Trust in God* for all things, and in this case for finances. As quickly as I had the thought, *Trust in God,* bam, I could feel a release from my body. I had kicked the devil out. This happened so quickly because of the persistency of prayer before my mind started to wander. I then had a dream. In it was of a man of power, or so he made himself out to be. His body was fairly large. He was like a bad father-in-law figure, someone who thinks he has some level of authority over you when they in fact do not. I looked directly at him with the same focus I had used when I was awake. With the authority given to me by God my stare caused the man to withdraw. He then disappeared. What was left was a poisonous snake, like a rattlesnake, retreating into a hole in the ground where the man had stood so it could hide. Less than a foot away there was another hole and I could see the front portion of its body passing through. The snake could also pop up again at this second hole if it chose to do so. Just as its tail portion was sliding underground, I quickly reached down with my left hand and grabbed the snake. Firmly grasping the snake's body I began to pull it backwards, out of the hole. I then recalled what Saint Paul had done on the island of Malta when his ship had shipwrecked there in a storm on his way to Rome.

In **Acts 28:3-6** Luke wrote, *"As Paul gathered an armful of sticks and was laying them on the fire, a poisonous snake, driven out by the heat, bit him on the hand. The people of the island saw it hanging from his hand and said to each other, "A murderer, no doubt! Though he escaped the sea, justice will not permit him to live." But Paul shook off the snake into the fire and was unharmed. The people waited for him to swell up or suddenly drop dead. But when they had waited a long time and saw that he wasn't harmed, they changed their minds and decided he was a god."*

I continued to pull the snake out. As the snake's head began to appear, I reached down with my right hand and grabbed it just behind its head so that I could break its neck and kill him.

In this dream the large man represented the devil. He posed as if he had authority over me, when in fact he did not, and that he was a father-in-law like figure. This is interesting as the devil wants to be God, our Father, but he is not, so he pretends to be. The devil acts like he has power over us but he does not. Through my persistence and with authority as written in Luke 9:1, he quickly retreated and then turned into a snake. In Genesis the devil presented himself to Eve as a snake. In my dream the devil's true nature was exposed, that of a slithering snake, and he was retreating down into his hole. Even more interesting was the hole that the snake was retreating into. He could hide there and go unseen and unnoticed, a seemingly perfect hiding place. He would only come out when he could do harm to someone, and only then when we unwittingly invite him with a sinful thought or deed.

While awake immediately before this dream, and having been focused and persistent in pursuing the devil, and then having the thought of having Trust in God, I was able to cause the devil to retreat. I also discovered his hiding place. I then removed him from my being, as seen in the dream.

Preparing for the Body of Christ

While giving the Eucharist the Catholics believe that they in essence are traveling through time, either going back to the Last Supper, or bringing that reality forward to the present. This sort of "time travel" is important for obvious reasons, that being to receive the Body of Christ in the present. What may not be so obvious is that we must do the same with how John the Baptist prepared for the coming of Christ. Christ is coming in His Body, which is the Church.

In 1 **Corinthians 12:27** Paul wrote, "*All of you together are Christ's body, and each of you is a part of it.*"

And from Luke **3:16 NLT.** Speaking of John the Baptist, John answered their questions by saying, *"I baptize you with water; but someone is coming soon who is greater than I am—so much greater that I'm not even worthy to be his slave and untie the straps of his sandals. He will baptize you with the Holy Spirit and with fire."*

To prepare the way for Christ, God sent John the Baptist. Without John the Baptist doing his work Christ would not have been able to come, as this was God's plan. We must now do the same to make way for the Body of Christ. We can mystically bring the work of John the Baptist forward by transporting our spiritual self to that time. We then bring ourselves back with that essence. This is not done in our physical bodies, at least not now, but with our minds in complete union with our spirit. By coming back to the present and with bringing that energy with us, which can all happen in a split second, we are in effect preparing for the coming of the Body of Christ.

Bilocation

Transporting oneself through time will sound odd to many Christians. However, such topics have been around since the beginnings of the church. Equally unusual is the topic of bilocation. This chapter emphasizes that knowledge with faith gives ability. In my dream of the Earth Splitting I described how I was in two places at one time. At some point in time I learned that this is what is called bilocation. I was surprised when I discovered that the Catholics have known of this phenomenon for hundreds of years, as many of their most devoted friars and priests are on the official record for having bilocated. The most recent example that I found was Padre Pio who lived from 1887 until 1968. He had numerous bilocation experiences where legitimate witnesses gave their testimony. It was determined that he was indeed seen in two locations miles apart at the same time.

The most interesting one that I found was that during WWII when American bombers were ordered to bomb the city of San Giovanni Rotondo. When the pilots got over the city a brown-robed friar appeared floating in the air in front of their aircraft. All attempts to release the bombs failed. Later on, an American air base was established at Foggia. One of the pilots went to San Giovanni and when he saw Padre Pio, he recognized him as being the one he saw before his aircraft. There are many others accounts that involved Padre Pio. Others who are known for their bilocation are Saint Drogo in the late 1100's, Saint Gerard Majella in the mid 1700's, and Saint John Bosco in the late

1880's. As I read in a Catholic publication, "This information proves to be of great wonder and edification to those who study them." I agree and the greater the knowledge we have of the universe and how God created it, the better ability we have to free ourselves. And the freer we are, the better chances we have to help free the billion souls.

Pros and Cons of Organized Religion

During the radio show that Bart and I did we spent one entire program discussing the pros and cons of organized religion. While on the air, I made the statement that the good news is that there is organized religion, and the bad news that there is organized religion. It is good news as it keeps the concept of God alive from generation to generation. The bad news is that too often those who are promoting God have gone off in their own direction, teaching a watered down and indoctrinated version. This has, as I have previously said, chased more people away from Christ than brought them to Christ. This is particularly true with many of the thirty-three thousand different Protestant denominations. However, I will say, talking about God and Christ in an often misinformed version is better than not talking about God at all.

I did have an interesting dream-vision on this subject. A loved one was interested in the Greek

Orthodox Church, so I went to mass with him a few times. Later on, I had a dream- like vision where we were standing in the inside of the church. The walls were such that you could see through them, or better said, around the main structural components of the walls. From inside I could see the outside courtyard and the people in it. What I was seeing was in fact Heaven, and that the Orthodox church did provide the means to see into Heaven. This is a good thing, though I could not go and experience Heaven, as there were limitations to the church and I could not get past its walls.

What I have found is that most churches that I have gone to insist that their version of understanding and interpreting the Bible is the right way, and that those who disagree are wrong. I suppose that I could argue this as well, if I were to state that my way of becoming to know God is the right way. But that is silly as I know many people who know God in their own way and I believe they know him well. I also believe it is essential that when praying to God, talking to God, and finding your own spirituality it must feel natural. It must be the Greater You that is guiding you. Remember, God talks to us through our spirit. You will know when you feel it, as there is nothing else like it.

For example, recently I was listening to a YouTube of perhaps my most favorite preacher. He was teaching on how the laws of God work.

Later, I tried adhering to his way on this particular subject but it just did not seem right. Then I thought back to the time when I went through the nine steps, I was so very ill, and yet I made it through without any religion. I went by what felt natural, to when God was guiding me. This is what works.

Yet There Are Those Who Refuse To Believe

Sadly, no matter how much evidence is provided there are those who refuse to believe. I have found that they simply will not listen. They take your words and translate them differently such that it will fit their own narrative of life. They accuse you of being a fanatic and lump you in with every other person that has come knocking on their door wanting to talk about God. What can we do? Nothing, just emanate as much love as possible.

Chapter Nine

Knowing God and God's Love

1 Corinthians 8:1. Paul says when speaking about food that has been offered to idols, *"Yes, we know that "we all have knowledge" about this issue. But while knowledge makes us feel important, it is love that strengthens the church ... but the person who loves God is the one whom God recognizes."*

You now have enough knowledge to seal off and cast out the enemies access. For me, and for Jackson as far as that goes, I found that my personality glitches and any lingering insecurities had greatly diminished. I once had a client that was getting upset with me over the phone because the drawings for his project were late. I actually had little if anything to do with the completion date of these particular drawings, but this client was releasing his frustration onto me. This was a while back and I would like to think I am further along now than I was then. During the conversation I had closed off all access that the enemy might find to influence my emotions. Yet, once again, I recognized that gut feeling of the insecurity when it came to wanting approval and avoiding conflict.

I ended up solving the client's problem rather quickly and all parties were happy. Nonetheless, I did not like the fact that the insecurity inside of me was still present. I asked myself, knowing that it first appeared when I was a young child, "What is it you are looking for?" Automatically I thought, *Love!*

Just as quickly as I had the thought, I then placed love directly on to the emotion of wanting approval, in my solar plexus area. The feeling went away! If you think about it this makes perfect sense. As small children we seek love from our parents. If we do not get it, or mistakenly think we do not have it, we get upset. We then adapt a behavior that we think will get us that love. As adults we no longer rely on love from our parents in that manner. And when we learn how we can simply put that love onto ourselves.

This was the very first message that my spirit gave to me when I heard, "Brent, it is okay to love yourself." Here it is Love that is the ultimate answer. This is very important to understand.

A person can learn to place love, non-narcissistic love as described in Lesson Two, onto their self. The benefits in doing so are many. However, emanating Gods love, or agape love, onto others takes a lot more practice. I once heard a preacher state that we cannot emanate agape love while we are in our bodies here on Earth. I would like to think that this is not true. However, there are far and few between that I have met that I felt like they were in fact emanating God's love. Yet Jesus certainly did, and he did so when I felt him next to my bedside, as previously described.

When I felt Jesus' presence next to me I recall thinking, *I have never felt love like this before.* The good news is I had the wonderful experience of having felt God's love. The bad news is, honestly, I have not yet achieved that level of love for others. I certainly have emotional love for my family and friends, but not the kind of love that Jesus had. This is okay, as if I could, I would have already achieved what Paul said in Ephesians 4, that being we are to meet the full and complete standards of Christ.

Speaking of love, when it comes to romantic love the one thing that I have learned, which actually came to me through my spirit many years ago, is that what women want is love, but what men want is freedom. And that men cannot fully give that love until they are fully given their freedom. Of course, it is best to define the word "freedom." It does not mean to be

227

promiscuous or commit adultery. A man mature in his spirituality would never do that. But the woman cannot try and control the man from doing that, as then she had not given him his freedom. Mutual trust and respect are key to a relationship whereby a complete understanding of love and freedom is achieved.

I do not believe we as men can fully obtain the freedom we desire, without fully expressing ourselves. As stated in the earlier chapters, self-expression is a key element. It will help us to do our role in the freeing of the one billion souls. From May of 2019 through December of that year Bart Chapman, my co-host, and I aired our radio show, "The Freeing of One Billion Souls." In it we discussed the nine lessons described in the first few chapters of this book and then went on to talk further about God. Our discussion, of course, included delving into Ephesians 4 where Paul said we are to eventually meet the full and complete standards of Christ. We also discussed the pros and cons of organized religion, Christian mysticism, the battle in the Heavenly realms, and much more. All of this was a wonderful and fulfilling experience. There is nothing greater than self-expressing about God. And in doing so may we all come to know and learn to emanate God's love.

About the Author

Brent G. Maupin, P.E. is a licensed Civil Engineer and Architect in Arizona where he has practiced since 1993. He has felt a strong calling from the universal force that we call God for over the past thirty years. He has studied many world religions, ultimately concluding that we are to become like Christ. He was host to the Phoenix, AZ radio show "The Freeing of One Billion Souls," based on his book and spiritual experiences. He has also written and recorded over 30 songs including "In Touch With My Soul," which was the theme song to his radio show. For more information, visit his webpage at www.TheFreeingofOneBillionSouls.com.

Made in the USA
Middletown, DE
05 August 2021